INSIDE

ANNUAL 2019!

BUILD YOUR ULTIMATE PLAYER 38

SALAH v MBAPPE

MOHAMED SALAH and KYLIAN MBAPPE shone on the world stage in 2018 and now they're ready to take over the footy world! We check out the two stars to see who'll be the boss of 2018!

SUPERSTAR SHOWDOWN 4

FOOTY FASHION FAILS!

These superstars definitely won't make it onto the MATCH catwalk!

BONKERS PICS 36

THE HIGHEST RATED FIFA TEAM EVER!

BEST FIFA TEAM EVER 82

CRISTIANO RONALDO

RECORD-CHASER!

CR7's mega move to Juventus has given him the chance to set some huge footy records! Check out the ace stats he's aiming to reach in 2019!

INTERNATIONAL FOOTY IN 2019!

RONALDO'S RECORDS 8

SUPER SALAH

£34 million seemed a bit pricy for Salah when he joined Liverpool, but after owning the Prem and Champions League, he's easily worth five times as much now! He broke tons of records on his way to lifting the Prem Golden Boot and now he's ready to lift some serious silverware!

TOP 2019 TARGET

Going one better in the Champions League would be class, but Liverpool fans really want to get their hands on the Premier League. They've waited almost 30 years since their last title!

MO'S 2018 IN NUMBERS

10	32	28
Hit ten goals on his way to the Champions League final!	Bagged the Prem Golden Boot with 32 goals!	First Egyptian to score a World Cup goal in 28 years!

STAT ATTACK!

Salah, Mane and Firmino all bagged double figures in the 2017-18 CL – the first trio from one club to do so!

STAR SUPPORT

Salah gets huge help from his strike partners. Sadio Mane's pace makes him super dangerous, while Roberto Firmino knits The Reds' attacks together with his movement. Plus, they do loads of defensive work too, so all Mo has to worry about is busting the net!

TOP SKILLS

- ✓ AWESOME ACCELERATION
- ✓ LETHAL LEFT FOOT
- ✓ DEMON DRIBBLING

BAPPE

MBAPPE'S THE MAN

There's no doubt Mbappe has the potential to be one of the best footballers in the world for years to come. His performances at the World Cup proved he's already good enough to mix it at the top of the game - and he's only going to get better!

TOP 2019 TARGET

Even though they've got an epic XI, PSG still haven't properly challenged for the Champo League! They need to beat the best - and Mbappe could just make the difference for them!

KYLIAN'S 2018 IN NUMBERS

£165.7M	2	60
Became the most expensive teenager ever!	Lifted his second Ligue 1 title in a row!	First teen to score in the World Cup final for 60 years!

STAT ATTACK!

Mbappe, Neymar and Cavani helped PSG score 108 goals in 2017-18 – their highest Ligue 1 tally ever!

STAR SUPPORT

Mbappe's the youngest member of PSG's lethal MCN attack, but he's equally as important! Combining his pace with Neymar's unreal skill and Edinson Cavani's clever movement makes the trio deadly!

TOP SKILLS

- ✓ MIND-BLOWING SPEED
- ✓ FIRST-CLASS FINISHING
- ✓ DEVASTATING DRIBBLING

THE £1 BILLION TEAM!

After last summer's transfers, it's now possible to build a realistic footy XI worth over £1 billion in combined transfer fees for the first time ever! Check out this mega money line-up...

DEMBELE
Barcelona
£96.8 million

POGBA
Man. United
£89 million

MBAPPE
PSG
£165.7 million

RONALDO
Juventus
£99.2 million

MBAPPE

Even PSG couldn't afford to buy Neymar and Mbappe in the same summer, so the young gun joined them on loan from Monaco for a year. The French champions completed the deal during the World Cup, coughing up the second biggest transfer fee ever!

TOTAL VALUE:
£1.05 BILLION

THE FOOTBALL £££££££££ RICH LIST!

According to Forbes, these are the most valuable footy clubs in the world!

1

MAN. UNITED
Value: £3.16 billion

2

REAL MADRID
Value: £3.14 billion

KEPA

KEPA
Chelsea
£71.6 million

Just a couple of weeks after Liverpool shattered the world transfer record for a goalkeeper by forking out nearly £67 million on Alisson, Chelsea trumped their rivals with the signing of Kepa Arrizabalaga from Athletic Bilbao. Wow!

WALKER
Man. City
£45 million

VAN DIJK
Liverpool
£75 million

LAPORTE
Man. City
£57 million

MENDY
Man. City
£52 million

COUTINHO
Barcelona
£105 million

NEYMAR
PSG
£198 million

DANNY ROSE

The England and Spurs left-back's little brother **MITCH ROSE** plays for League Two Grimsby! Rose Jr. can also play at full-back, but prefers central midfield!

HARRY MAGUIRE

Another player who's followed in his brother's footsteps to play footy is **LAURENCE MAGUIRE**. Harry's little bro is also a CB and plays for National League side Chesterfield!

ALEX OXLADE-CHAMBERLAIN

The Ox's dad **MARK CHAMBERLAIN** won eight caps for England back in the 1980s and his little brother Christian is a midfielder for Notts County!

NATHANIEL CHALOBAH

Brothers Nathaniel and **TREVOH CHALOBAH** both came through the Chelsea academy and have won over 100 England youth caps between them. Sick!

NEYMAR

PSG changed footy forever when they paid almost £200 million for Neymar in 2017! The Brazilian's Barcelona buy-out clause was supposed to put clubs off ever trying to sign him, but the Parisians stumped up the cash anyway!

LAPORTE

When Man. City signed Laporte in January 2018, they completed the most expensive defence ever with the solid Frenchman alongside Benjamin Mendy, Kyle Walker and John Stones. The four cost more than £200 million combined!

3

BARCELONA
Value: £3.11 billion

4
BAYERN MUNICH
Value: £2.35 billion

5

MAN. CITY
Value: £1.89 billion

CRISTIANO

RECORD-CHASER!

CR7's mega move to Juventus has given him the chance to set some huge footy records! Check out the ace stats he's aiming to reach in 2019...

3

He could match Clarence Seedorf's record as being the only player to win the CL with three different clubs!

600

If he can hit 27 goals for Juventus, he'll reach 600 in all competitions in club football!

100

A century of international goals is in his sights as well. The all-time record is 109!

MICHY'S MEGA FAIL!

World Cup 2018 totally rocked, but our highlight was still Michy Batshuayi booting a ball off the post and into his own face. LOL!

50 CLUB!

In 2019, if a Championship team achieves promotion to the Prem for the first time ever, they'll become the 50th club to play in the Premier League!

RONALDO

5

He could match Messi's record for European Golden Shoes and become the first player to win it with three different teams!

10

Nobody's scored more CL goals against one team than Ron's ten against Juventus, but he could beat his own record this year – he's got nine against Bayern!

6

Only one player in history has won six Champo Leagues – and CR7 is just one behind!

1

Nobody's ever won the Premier League, La Liga and Serie A titles. Ronaldo could become the first!

8

Cristiano's already won more CL Golden Boots than anyone else, but is chasing the award for the eighth time. Mad!

INTERNATIONAL FOOTY IN 2019!

There's no World Cup or Euros, but these tournaments will defo be worth watching!

ASIAN CUP
January–February

South Korea, Japan, Iran and Australia gave us tons of entertainment during the World Cup in Russia!

U20 WORLD CUP
May–June

England won't be there to defend their trophy, but there will still be loads of talent on show in Poland!

COPA AMERICA
June

South America's finest head to Brazil this summer! Can Messi finally get his hands on an international trophy?

AFCON
June

The Africa Cup Of Nations will be hosted by Cameroon in the summer so it doesn't clash with the Prem!

U21 EUROS
June

Europe's top wonderkids go head-to-head in Italy and San Marino in June. Can Germany retain their title?

GOLD CUP
June–July

USA will have a big point to prove as hosts of this tournament after missing out on World Cup 2018!

U17 WORLD CUP
October

England won this awesome tournament in India back in 2017. Can The Young Lions repeat the trick in Peru?

BALLON D'OR DEFENDERS

The Ballon d'Or award has been around since 1956, but only three defenders have ever won it!

FRANZ BECKENBAUER
Germany • 1972 & 1976

MATTHIAS SAMMER
Germany • 1996

FABIO CANNAVARO
Italy • 2006

BEAT THAT, CR7!

Money Bags ME$$I!

LIONEL MESSI pocketed over £80m in salary and endorsements last year, making him the second-highest earning sportsman in the world behind boxing legend Floyd Mayweather!

MATCH!
THE BEST FOOTBALL MAGAZINE!

Fab Fact

Auba' brothers Willy and Catilina came through AC Milan's youth academy alongside him!

Boots

Nike Hypervenom

Stat Attack

Aubameyang's scored over 0 goals in all comps in each of his last three seasons!

Transfer Value

£65 million

AUBAMEYANG

LA LIGA GOAL KING
MESSI

For the last ten years, La Liga's crown for best goal king has been passed back and forth from Messi to Cristiano Ronaldo, but the Portugal legend's departure means it belongs to Leo now. The Barcelona man has earned it, too! Here's why he's the king of goalscoring in La Liga...

GOALSCORING GAME

✓ Messi's left foot is absolutely deadly. When he gets a chance in or around the penalty box, keepers have no chance!

✓ Some players panic under pressure, but Leo's ridiculously calm. He takes his time, picks his spot and takes his chances!

✓ He wouldn't get as many chances without his insane dribbling ability. Messi dances through defences to line up shots for fun!

GOAL NO.1

When a 17-year-old kid came off Barça's bench at home to Albacete in May 2005, nobody knew they were about to see history being made. Within minutes of coming on as a sub for Samuel Eto'o, Leo ran onto a class Ronaldinho lobbed through ball and cheekily chipped the keeper. A legend was born!

Club: Barcelona
Country: Argentina
Age: 31
Height: 5ft 7in
Boots: adidas Nemeziz

FACTPACK!

LA LIGA RECORDS

8 Most hat-tricks in a season

21 Longest scoring streak

50 Most goals in a season

383 All-time La Liga top scorer

BEST SEASON

At the start of 2011-12, Leo had already won two Ballons d'Or and three Champo League titles, but his top-scoring season was yet to come. His form that year was unbelievable. With Xavi, Andres Iniesta and Dani Alves in support, he netted an incredible 50 goals – including eight hat-tricks and seven braces – and averaged a goal every 65 minutes. Mad!

LAST SEASON

It says everything about Leo that despite scoring 34 league goals and creating 12 more, winning the Pichichi and European Golden Shoe, and lifting the La Liga title, he still wanted more from 2017-18! Barça's quarter-final exit in the Champions League and their unbeaten season coming to an end in the second-last game took the gloss off a brilliant campaign, but the No.10 showed he's still as good as ever. Legend!

RIVAL FOR THE THRONE

Antoine Griezmann

Leo has spent most of his career battling with CR7 for top spot in La Liga, but that's changed now. World Cup winner Griezmann's left foot is just as good, but he's never scored more than 22 goals in a season. He needs to improve that big-time to take the throne!

GREATEST GOAL

Real Madrid	2	3	Barcelona

April 23, 2017 You could spend all day watching Messi's best goals, but this one's our fave. Bagging a last-minute winner, his 500th Barça goal of his career, at the home of their biggest rivals? Sweet!

Stats correct up to start of the 2018-19 season.

ULTIMATE GUIDE TO...
SESSEGNON!

MATCH tells you everything you need to know about one of the world's brightest young football talents – and a future ENGLAND megastar in the making!

FAST FACTS

RECORD-BREAKER
Sess was the first player born in the 21st century in England, the youngest player ever to net in the Championship and is one of the FA Cup's youngest ever scorers too!

FOOTY FAMILY
Ryan's twin brother Steven also plays for Fulham, and distant cousin Stephane played almost 200 Prem games for West Brom and Sunderland between 2010 and 2016. Class!

PFA PRO
In 2017-18, he became the first non-Prem player ever to be nominated for the PFA Young Player Of The Year award! He bagged a record five personal gongs at the EFL Awards too!

PROMOTION HERO
Fulham wouldn't have reached the Prem without Sessegnon - he scored one and created another in the play-off semi-final, before bagging another assist in the final. What a legend!

2017-18 STATS
Games: 52
Goals: 16
Assists: 8

PACE TO BURN
Some players have lightning acceleration, others are quick over long distances and some have to slow down massively when dribbling, but Sessegnon is just pure pace! He explodes away from defenders with the ball in the blink of an eye - and once he gets going, nobody can catch him!

FACTPACK!
Club: Fulham
Age: 18
Position: Left winger /Left-back
Boots: Nike Phantom VSN

VERSATILITY

Ryan's got attention for his goals and assists, but he's played a lot in defence too. Because he's so good going forward, he's a real attacking threat from left-back, but he's also so quick he hardly ever gets caught out of position. He could take over as England's left wing-back very soon!

DETERMINATION

Sess almost always has an impact on the game because of his attitude. When he has the ball he tries to run at his marker straight away, and when he doesn't he busts a gut to get into the penalty area. Most of his goals usually come from a direct dribble and shot or getting on the end of a cross!

IS HE THE NEXT... GARETH BALE?

As a rapid, teenage left-back who took the Championship by storm and was pushed forward to unlock his attacking potential, Ryan and Gaz's early careers are almost identical! If he carries on, Sess will become the best player in the Prem before sealing a world-record transfer! Don't rule it out!

RYAN'S ROUTE!

RYAN SESSEGNON tells MATCH all about his path to the Premier League!

STARTING OUT...

RYAN SAYS: "Me and my brother started at a local Sunday league team, just playing for fun. We were seen by Fulham and went down for a trial, did well and progressed into the academy from the Under-9s!"

JOINING FULHAM...

RYAN SAYS: "I don't remember too much about it – I was just really excited to be joining an academy. My aim was to see how well I could do in an academy and how I could progress as a young player. I played everywhere basically, but I always tried to push on and attack!"

SCHOOL DAYS...

RYAN SAYS: "I was more worried about playing football! Our school team had lots of Fulham players, so we had a good chemistry and that made us even stronger. We won two national cup finals and it'll always stand out in my mind. To do it with friends was special!"

ENGLAND GLORY...

RYAN SAYS: "Going into the Under-19 Euros we were confident – we knew we'd win it! In the final we played a strong Portugal team so I was more nervous, but we'd already beaten everyone else. When I heard the final whistle and we'd won 2-1, we fell to our knees with relief. I can't describe the feeling – it was amazing!"

TOP ADVICE...

RYAN SAYS: "Work hard, never give up and just enjoy your football!"

NOW TURN OVER FOR MORE ENGLAND WONDERKIDS!

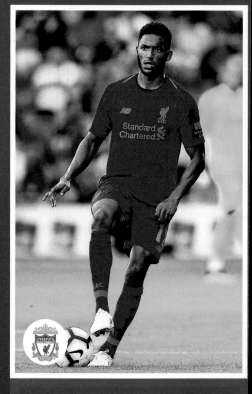

PHIL FODEN

Position: Attacking midfielder
Age: 18 ★ Man. City

Man. City coaches had been whispering about a red-hot academy prospect for a while before Foden showed off his epic talent at the 2017 Under-17 World Cup! The wicked wonderkid totally dominated the tournament, following the likes of Cesc Fabregas and Toni Kroos by winning the Golden Ball, and scored twice in the final!

IS HE THE NEXT... LIONEL MESSI?

It's a huge shout to compare anyone with Leo, but the little left-footed Foden looks just like Messi when he sets off on a mazy dribble on the edge of the penalty box!

JADON SANCHO

Position: Winger
Age: 18 ★ Borussia Dortmund

Like Foden, Sancho was another product of Man. City's academy, but he left before making his City debut. Dortmund snapped him up after selling Ousmane Dembele to Barça, and he's quickly established himself as one of the highest-rated young players in the Bundesliga - he got one goal and four assists in just seven starts last season!

IS HE THE NEXT... EDEN HAZARD?

Sancho has bags of pace, tons of tekkers and loves cutting in off the left wing to run at defenders, so epic Belgium baller Hazard is the perfect role model for him!

JOE GOMEZ

Position: Centre-back
Age: 21 ★ Liverpool

Defender Gomez would probably be an England regular by now if he hadn't picked up so many injuries. The Reds youngster bossed his first ever international start up against Brazil and Neymar, but missed the World Cup in Russia with an ankle problem. He's still really young though, and has the potential to become a Three Lions hero!

IS HE THE NEXT... RIO FERDINAND?

Ferdinand was one of the most talented and decorated English centre-backs ever, but Gomez reminds us of him with his pace and ability to bring the ball out of defence!

ERATION!

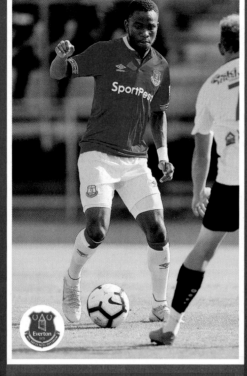

*On loan From Chelsea.

MASON MOUNT

Position: Attacking midfielder
Age: 19 ★ Derby*

Chelsea's academy stars haven't found it easy to break into the club's first team over the years, but we'd be shocked if Mount doesn't go on to have a serious career at Stamford Bridge. He fired England to glory at the Under-19 European Championship in 2017, before joining Dutch side Vitesse where he was named Player Of The Year!

IS HE THE NEXT… CHRISTIAN ERIKSEN?

Just like the Denmark legend, Mount bags loads of assists thanks to his creativity, crossing and dead-ball deliveries! He's also got the flair to dribble around defenders!

ADEMOLA LOOKMAN

Position: Winger
Age: 20 ★ Everton

We couldn't believe Everton let Lookman go out on loan to RB Leipzig in January 2018 - the rapid winger has tons of talent! The Toffees paid Charlton £11 million to sign him 12 months earlier, but he headed to Germany to get some regular first-team action - and became the first Englishman to score in the Bundesliga since 2005!

IS HE THE NEXT… RAHEEM STERLING?

Lookman loves running at defenders and cutting in from the wing to burst into the penalty box. Plus, he gets into some great goalscoring positions, just like Sterling!

UK & IRELAND YOUNG GUNS!

The rest of the United Kingdom and Ireland has sick talents too!

KIERAN TIERNEY

Scotland & Celtic

Tierney is a boyhood Celtic supporter that's living the dream as one of their star players! He's got everything needed to be a world class left-back. Ledge!

†On loan from Liverpool.

BEN WOODBURN

Wales & Sheffield United†

Forward Woodburn has already had a big impact on Wales' first team after scoring an absolute screamer against Austria in a World Cup qualifier!

PAUL SMYTH

Northern Ireland & QPR

The awesome young striker scored on his QPR debut in January 2018, before doing the same for his national team just two months later. He's gonna go far!

MICHAEL OBAFEMI

Rep. Of Ireland & Southampton

Southampton's second youngest Prem player ever has big talent! He's already played for the Ireland U19s, but spies say England and Nigeria are also sniffing around!

BIG MATCH! QUIZ

PREMIER LEAGUE SPECIAL

Andreas Christensen

James Milner

Victor Moses

Jamie Vardy

Phil Jones

Danny Welbeck

ODD ONE OUT!

Which of these players has never won the Premier League title?

FLIPPED!

Which Prem superstar has had his face messed up in this weird pic?

CRAZY KIT!

Which side wore this eye-busting orange third kit in 2008-09?

MEGA MASH-UP!

Can you name the rock-solid CB in this mega blurry shot?

STADIUM GAME

Match these grounds to the 2018-19 Prem clubs that play there!

Molineux	Amex	St. Mary's	Craven Cottage
1	**2**	**3**	**4**

A	B	C	D
Brighton	Southampton	Fulham	Wolves

SPOT THE BALL!

Mark where you think the ball is in this cool action pic!

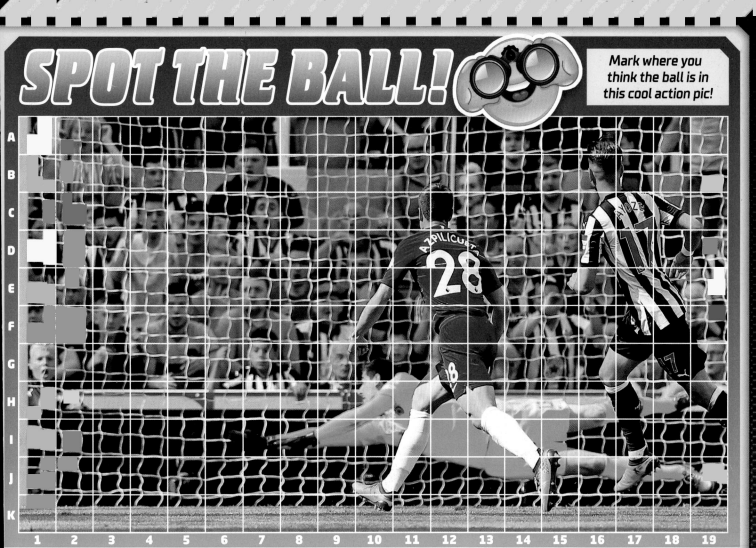

A B C D E F G H I J K

1 2 3 4 5 6 7 8 9 10 11 12 13 14 15 16 17 18 19

2012-13

2013-14

GUESS THE WINNERS!

Do you know which clubs won the Prem in these seasons?

2014-15

2015-16

World-Class Keepers!

Name the clubs these GKs play for!

1. Nick Pope

2. Jordan Pickford

3. Wayne Hennessey

4. Asmir Begovic

5. David De Gea

6. Hugo Lloris

MATCH! WINNER!

Who scored Tottenham's winner against Arsenal in last season's North London derby at Wembley?

ANSWERS ON PAGE 91

MEGA WORDSEARCH

Can you find the legendary Prem heroes in this giant grid?

```
S T V I C X I                              L D E K C H B
E A N E L K A                              I P N T R R L
H V J R E E L                              D R L N J Q L
I K P Q R A B                              O J X P R Z Y
J R A A H Y O R K D G N D F F Z Z V G V H M L S W E K I E N G A
Q Z F R A N K M I R L I B E V R V Z Y D J X C F Y J B I S N B L
D X A E S L N G N G D Z W J E B X R N E M P B F C Z S E B W U O
H S A U S C Z P G M G X E H V V O K O C H A G D I S R B W O O N
E P D C E J X X B Y Q K G X R A N C E S N C O D I O N E V U U S
W B B M L S S K K U F A F D K Y R H V J D E S T M Y X R Y Z D O
L Z W N B S Y B V W R U I U N U B J H W A N E Y C Y C G I Y B F
P O O I A L N B O R P A D R Q E Y D G H U L L D Q X L K P I N B
O P B G I W E B A H X I V N B Y O N H E G L R I C O B A C G V J
Y P I U N U P C E P V A X E D X T Z D D O S N S R S K M Z A J I
E I E L K R C R Z C B P O I F S G N P C R P U T O N H P Q H Q G
T J J C A N T O N A K X Z L Q F A X T Q U O C I O P D E K M Q M
P J U J U L N Y H H V H I N Y T S S W X D Z G N R R N C A P U P
E I N N E E D E V Q Q F A Z H S C J H J T R K B Y X K P G R E Q
Y W I U C U T T J D S R K M I D O S J R A O A F A T W E Y X E Q
Q O N E F X E G J J V W H L I I I O A L F O I G N W Q U R P Q R
N P H Z E H W R U K A V D I S C G Y H Y N N Y Y U Q S J H D F L
S N O Y R P Y L H R O Q Z T Q A N P G I W E S Z S G S E D S Q E
X O C O D R M Z Q W P P M B T N E Q S X G Y J F G Q D S H M V
B X R Y I Z A U G F L N X W U I T X G K U N N I A L B F M E A L
S J O W N I N Z N S A P Q F T O Y U M E U W G B G W M Z F R L H
Q E V H A C F O W L E R H A A D B K Y A Q F H I N N K U D I X E
T R C E N T W Y D N J G L O B S V Y N N A T P A C W C Z N N S N
X S X T D E E Q T G Z N A T H Y C N T E M H G N E P F T L G P R
L X B X L K K W M D O L I L R X N H F I S O K A F X S P Q H B Y
S S L P S X E C R S O W C S A P Q M M L I C I Y P Z D W X A L K
A Y T E I K C A U N G A D K L M M D A E I J U G O S Q X W M I P
B I H D D E R G I V A K Z V K P P R H R I E O Z P E U U G L G D
J B G J H R R G S N T E Q B P Q I A R B D C A S O B F L N V M B
P J K N E E L K F S I W O K B E G A R P H T H B J L J U V U C
X P B G F R L V G U S J K W I L C B N D R W C E M U A D X H C G
N H V H S K T E K A T Z F V E T D R I D W I S F L X T X S O Z M
Z B B I M H M W A N C H O P E N Z J Q Q O N S U G J K N D L S P
L M G X C A H I L L K S C H W A R Z E R V C G Y C T H L E D Q Q
U Z U S Y G W S R T L I T M A N E N N W T K L A N V Q O I L S Z
```

Alonso	Cantona	Distin	Gascoigne	Henry	Lampard	Poyet	Sheringham
Anelka	Carragher	Drogba	Gerrard	Heskey	Le Tissier	Rooney	Viduka
Beckham	Carrick	Ferdinand	Giggs	Juninho	Litmanen	Schwarzer	Vieira
Bergkamp	Collymore	Ferguson	Ginola	Keane	Okocha	Schmeichel	Wanchope
Cahill	Di Canio	Fowler	Hasselbaink	King	Owen	Shearer	Zola

ANSWERS ON PAGE 94

MATCH!
THE BEST FOOTBALL MAGAZINE!

NEYMAR

Fab Fact

Neymar shattered the world transfer record when he joined PSG for £198 million in 2017!

Boots

Nike Mercurial

Stat Attack

He's one of only four players to score over 50 goals for Brazil!

Transfer Value

£200 million

SNAPPED!
BEST OF 2018!

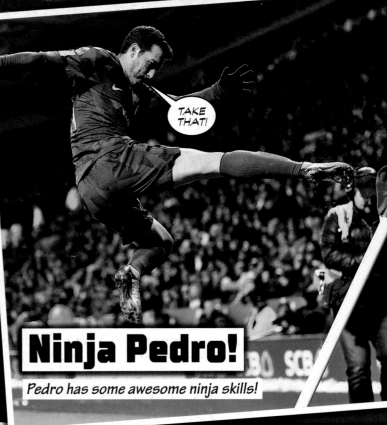

Ninja Pedro!

> TAKE THAT!

Pedro has some awesome ninja skills!

G.O.A.T!

One's an animal and one's the greatest player of all time...

> NO, YOU'RE THE ANIMAL!

Hi-tech specs!

> WHERE'S THE BALL?

Jonjo left his real glasses at home!

> PLEASE LET ME DOWN!

Sergio Potter.

Ramos is a real-life magician on the footy pitch!

Bench warmers!

Face-plant!

The Levante GK needed plastic surgery for this one!

Man. City CBs Stones and Laporte share everything!

Walker fountain!

How lifelike is this Kyle Walker water fountain?

Poch's Haka!

The Spurs boss tried out some new tactics!

Job swap!

The Chelsea stars decided to give photography a go!

Gloves prank!

Someone stuck Super Glue to Adrian's gloves!

THE MATCH BOOK OF...
FOOTY RECORDS

We reveal some of the most incredible records from the world of football!

THE LEGENDS!

The biggest and best records in world footy belong to this lot! Check it out...

50

Kazuyoshi Miura is football's oldest ever scorer aged 50! The previous record was held by England legend Stanley Matthews, but the Japan striker beat him by nine days!

1,390

Nobody has played more official games than legendary England goalkeeper Peter Shilton. He's also The Three Lions' most capped player with 125 appearances!

12

Mauricio Baldivieso made his debut for Bolivian side Aurora FC when he was just 12 years old! What!?

Welsh Premier League club The New Saints won 27 top-flight matches in a row in 2016 to set a new European record previously held by Ajax. Wowzers!

27

104

Romanian giants Steaua Bucharest hold the record for the longest unbeaten run in European history, going 104 games without defeat between 1986 and 1989!

38

The most decorated player ever is PSG star Dani Alves! The Brazilian has won a ridiculous 38 trophies during his career... and counting!

69

Scottish champions Celtic went a British record 69 consecutive matches unbeaten before their run was emphatically ended in a 4-0 defeat by Hearts in 2017!

THE FLOPS!

The holders of these records won't want to read this!

20

Sunderland hold the record for consecutive Premier League defeats! They lost 20 games in a row across two different seasons in 2002-03 and 2005-06!

46

We thought Real Madrid centre-back Sergio Ramos had seen red too many times, but retired Colombia midfielder Gerardo Bedoya is way ahead. He was sent off 46 times in his career!

14

In 2017, Italian side Benevento set the record for the worst start to a season in one of Europe's top five leagues. They lost 14 Serie A matches in a row!

10

Former Man. City defender Richard Dunne holds the record for Prem own goals. He got ten in total and only managed 11 at the right end!

3

Ex-Argentina striker Martin Palermo is the only player in international footy history to miss three penalties in one game – against Colombia in the 1999 Copa America. Fail!

The worst ever Prem team was Derby in 2007-08. They only won one game, lost 29 and ended the season with just 11 points!

11

THE GOALS!
These records are all about goals, goals, goals!

131

149

ADEMA A.S. AEROPORTS DE MADAGASCAR

STADE OLYMPIQUE DE L'ÉMYRNE
ARIVOLAHY TSY MATY INDRAY

The most goals ever in one match was in 2002 in Madagascar between SO l'Émyrne and AS Adema. SO l'Émyrne were so annoyed with past refereeing decisions, they slammed in 149 own goals in protest. Bonkers!

There's only one winner for the top-scoring GK ever! Brazilian set-piece specialist Rogerio Ceni bagged 61 free-kicks and 69 penalties in his career. Unbelievable!

13

91

850

Leo Messi scored 91 goals in all competitions for club and country in 2012 – the highest ever number in a single calendar year!

Loads of players claim to have scored the most goals ever, but the official title belongs to Austrian striker Josef Bican, who hit 805 in official matches between 1928 and 1955!

The highest-scoring international game ever was in 2001 between Australia and American Samoa. The Socceroos won 31-0, with striker Archie Thompson bagging 13!

2

109

The fastest goal ever was scored by Saudi Arabia forward Nawaf Al Abed. There were only two seconds on the clock when he smashed the ball in straight from the kick-off for Al Hilal v Al Shoalah in 2017!

Iran legend Ali Daei has scored more international goals than anyone else, although Cristiano Ronaldo started the 2018-19 season just 24 behind him!

THE ONE & ONLY!

These players all hold totally unique football records!

Ex-Iceland striker Eidur Gudjohnsen is the only player ever to replace his father during an international game. He was subbed on for dad Arnor in 1996!

Ex-Republic Of Ireland defender Steve Finnan is the only player ever to play in all four of England's top divisions, the Conference, Champo League, UEFA Cup, Intertoto Cup and World Cup!

Liverpool legend Steven Gerrard scored in the finals of the FA Cup, League Cup, Champo League and UEFA Cup – the only player ever to do so!

Gareth Bale is the only player to get a goal, assist, yellow card and own goal in one Premier League game – against Liverpool back in 2012!

Ex-Inter midfielder Dejan Stankovic has the honour of being the only player to go to three World Cups with three different countries – Yugoslavia, Serbia & Montenegro and Serbia!

Ex-Croatia CB Josip Simunic is the only player to get three yellow cards in one game! English ref Graham Poll had a nightmare at the 2006 World Cup before finally sending him off!

FOLLOW MATCH!

FOR LOADS OF AWESOME FOOTY NEWS, TRANSFER GOSSIP, VIDEOS & EPIC LOLS!

facebook.com/
matchmagazine

youtube.com/matchymovie

twitter.com/
matchmagazine

snapchat.com/add/
matchmagazine

instagram.com/
matchmagofficial

EPIC WEBSITE: WWW.MATCHFOOTBALL.CO.UK

HE SAID WHAT?

MATCH picks out its fave footy quotes from the 2017-18 season!

"I'M LIKE YOU, I'M AN ARSENAL FAN. THIS IS MORE THAN JUST WATCHING FOOTBALL, IT'S A WAY OF LIFE. I WOULD LIKE TO FINISH IN ONE SIMPLE SENTENCE – I WILL MISS YOU!"

Arsene Wenger's final speech as Arsenal boss was really emotional for Gunners fan

"I WILL LOOK TO THE LOBSTERS AND SEA BASS, BUT IF NOT WE MUST BUY SARDINES. BUT SOMETIMES SARDINES CAN WIN GAMES!"

Ex-Swansea gaffer Carlos Carvalhal comes out with some weird lines when talking about new signings!

"I'M THE BEST PLAYER IN HISTORY. I PLAY WELL WITH BOTH FEET, I'M QUICK, POWERFUL, GOOD WITH THE HEAD, I SCORE GOALS, I MAKE ASSISTS. THERE'S NO-ONE MORE COMPLETE THAN ME."

Cristiano Ronaldo was modest after winning the Ballon d'Or for the fifth time in 2017!

"I DIDN'T ACTUALLY EAT THE WORMS! YOU GET A NICE, BIG JUICY WORM HANGING OUT YOUR MOUTH AS IF YOU'RE CHEWING IT, THEN IT COMES OUT AND YOU WASH YOUR MOUTH OUT WITH WATER!"

Burnley boss Sean Dyche clears up a rumour about him worm-eating!

"THEY WON'T WIN 8-0. WHAT A STUPID QUESTION THAT IS. 8-0? WELL, NO I DON'T BELIEVE THAT."

Former Holland manager Dick Advocaat completely writes off Sweden hammering Luxembourg, before the Swedes do exactly that to end the Dutch's hopes of qualifying for the World Cup!

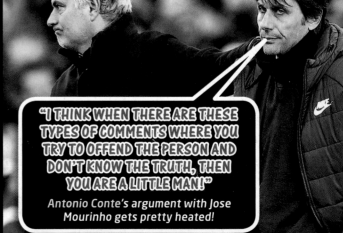

"I THINK WHEN THERE ARE THESE TYPES OF COMMENTS WHERE YOU TRY TO OFFEND THE PERSON AND DON'T KNOW THE TRUTH, THEN YOU ARE A LITTLE MAN!"

Antonio Conte's argument with Jose Mourinho gets pretty heated!

PREM GOAL KING
KANE

Kane's run of Premier League Golden Boot wins might have ended last season, but the England striker is still top dog when it comes to Prem centre-forwards. He's dreaming of breaking the league's all-time scoring record, but we reckon he's already the goal king! Here's why...

GOALSCORING GAME

✓ Kane spends hours working on his finishing, so his technique is absolutely flawless. When he takes a shot, it explodes off his foot!

✓ One of the reasons he scores so many goals is the number of shots he takes. Nobody had more attempts in the Prem than him in 2017-18!

✓ Harry's not one-footed either – more than half of his Premier League goals last season came from his left foot or with his head. Amazing!

GOAL NO.1

It seems only right that Kane's first Prem goal was assisted by Christian Eriksen – a player who's created loads for him since! Kane was already prolific in the Europa League, but had to wait until April 2014 to bag in the Prem. Latching onto a class cross from Eriksen, he tapped in to give Tottenham a 2-1 lead against Sunderland – and Harry hasn't looked back since!

BEST SEASON

When Kane picked up his first Golden Boot award, he still had his doubters who said he wasn't world class. All those critics were silenced in 2016-17, though – the Tottenham legend was unstoppable, scoring 29 goals in 30 games, including four hat-tricks, and fired Spurs to second in the league – their highest ever Prem finish!

FACTPACK!

Club: *Tottenham*
Country: *England*
Age: *25*
Height: *6ft 2in*
Boots: *Nike Hypervenom*

PREM RECORDS

0.97 Strike-rate for a Golden Boot winner

6 Hat-tricks in a calendar year

39 Goals in a calendar year

108 Tottenham's all-time top scorer

LAST SEASON

Kane beat his previous highest tally by one to score 30 goals in 2017-18. He missed out on the Prem Golden Boot though – for the first time since 2015 – but took his goalscoring to the highest level. Not only did he bag seven goals in seven Champo League matches, he finished top scorer at the 2018 World Cup, proving that he belongs among the very best strikers in the world!

GREATEST GOAL

Tottenham	2	2	Arsenal

March 5, 2016 Kane loves playing against Arsenal and this was his best goal in the derby. Dele Alli set it up with a sweet backheel, before Hazza smashed an unstoppable shot in from a really tight angle!

RIVAL FOR THE THRONE
Mohamed Salah

Mo arrived on the scene in 2017 and blew everyone away with his goalscoring form. It'll take more than one good season for the Egyptian to take the throne, but if he can bag over 30 goals again in 2018-19, Kane could be overtaken!

Stats correct up to the start of the 2018-19 season.

BIG MATCH! QUIZ

CHAMPIONS LEAGUE SPECIAL

Which Champions League goal king has decided to take up golf?

5 QUESTIONS ON...

BAYERN MUNICH

1 What is one of the Bundesliga champions' wicked nicknames – Star Of The South, Star Of The North or Star Of The West?

2 How many times have the German giants lifted the Champions League trophy – three, four, five or six?

3 True or False? Bayern won the 2013 Champions League Final against German rivals Borussia Dortmund!

4 What is the total stadium capacity of their mind-blowing Allianz Arena – under 70,000 or over 70,000?

5 What shirt number does defensive rock Mats Hummels wear for the German champions – No.3, No.4, No.5 or No.6?

1.

2.

CL SE-UP!

Which CL superstars have we zoomed in on?

3.

4.

SOCCER SCRABBLE

Rearrange these letters to figure out a past Champions League winning side!

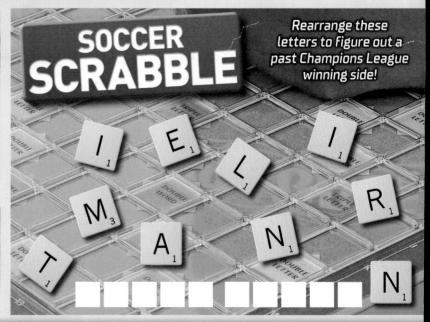

NAME THE TEAM!

Can you remember the Real Madrid XI that won the 2018 Champions League final?

Goalkeeper ★ Costa Rica	**KEYLOR NAVAS**
1. Centre-back ★ Spain	
2. Midfielder ★ Germany	
3. Centre-back ★ France	
4. Striker ★ France	
5. Forward ★ Portugal	
6. Midfielder ★ Brazil	
7. Left-back ★ Brazil	
8. Right-back ★ Spain	
9. Midfielder ★ Spain	
10. Midfielder ★ Croatia	

SUPER SKIPPERS!

C

Who are the captains of these 2018-19 CL clubs?

Roma

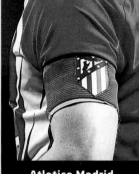

Atletico Madrid

Porto

Monaco

GOAL MACHINES!

Name the clubs these class forwards play for!

1. Kylian Mbappe

2. Mark Uth

3. Arkadiusz Milik

4. Edin Dzeko

5. Bertrand Traore

6. Marco Reus

MATCH! WINNER!

Who scored Liverpool's winner in their quarter-final second-leg clash against Man. City last season?

ANSWERS ON PAGE 94

SPOT THE STARS

Can you find 20 superstars from the 2017–18 CL season in this crowd?

1	JAMES MILNER	**6**	EDINSON CAVANI	**11**	DELE ALLI	**16**	NABY KEITA
2	CRISTIANO RONALDO	**7**	HARRY KANE	**12**	KEVIN DE BRUYNE	**17**	ALISSON
3	MOHAMED SALAH	**8**	LIONEL MESSI	**13**	GELSON MARTINS	**18**	MATS HUMMELS
4	WISSAM BEN YEDDER	**9**	GONZALO HIGUAIN	**14**	EDEN HAZARD	**19**	ALEKSANDAR KOLAROV
5	EDIN DZEKO	**10**	ROBERT LEWANDOWSKI	**15**	EVER BANEGA	**20**	MARLOS

ANSWERS ON PAGE 94

MATCH!
THE BEST FOOTBALL MAGAZINE!

Fab Fact

Reus has been named in the Bundesliga Team Of The Season on five occasions!

Boots

Puma Future

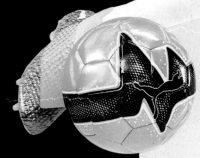

Stat Attack

The Dortmund and Germany hero has hit over 150 career goals for club and country!

Transfer Value

£50 million

REUS

NOT COOL, AUBA!

We really hope those glasses are a joke!

> I SEE YOU!

> THIS WORKS, RIGHT?

BUFF-WRONG!

Who said that Italians are fashion gurus?

KIMMICH'S GIMMICK!

Did Joshua buy that hat from a clown?

> VERY FUNNY, MATCH!

> YOU THINK I LOOK 'RUFF'?

TERRIBLE TRACKIE!

Did Aguero get dressed in the dark?

FASHION FAILS!

These superstars definitely won't make it onto the MATCH catwalk!

> YOU'RE JUST JEALOUS!

POG PAPPED!

You need sunglasses to look at those bottoms!

> I THINK THEY ROCK!

STERLING'S SHOCKER!

We're really not feeling those trousers, Raheem!

> I'M SO EDGY!

BELLERIN'S BLUNDER!

There's so much wrong with this outfit!

ULTIMATE

PLAYER!

MATCH picks out the best players on the planet to help create the world's ultimate footy star – then we want you to have your say for the chance to win an awesome prize!

PASSING

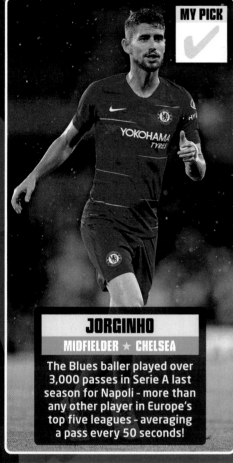

MY PICK ✔

JORGINHO
MIDFIELDER ★ CHELSEA

The Blues baller played over 3,000 passes in Serie A last season for Napoli - more than any other player in Europe's top five leagues - averaging a pass every 50 seconds!

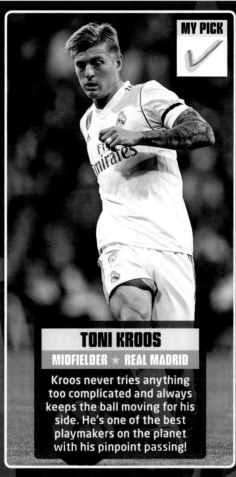

MY PICK ✔

TONI KROOS
MIDFIELDER ★ REAL MADRID

Kroos never tries anything too complicated and always keeps the ball moving for his side. He's one of the best playmakers on the planet with his pinpoint passing!

MY PICK ✔

MIRALEM PJANIC
MIDFIELDER ★ JUVENTUS

Pjanic hit 300 league passes more than any other Juventus player last season and totally dictates games for the Serie A champs. He always seems to know the best pass to make!

MY PICK ✔

SERGIO BUSQUETS
MIDFIELDER ★ BARCELONA

To play as the anchorman in a side that's philosophy is all about keeping the ball, you have to be a pass master! And of course, Busquets is one of the very best!

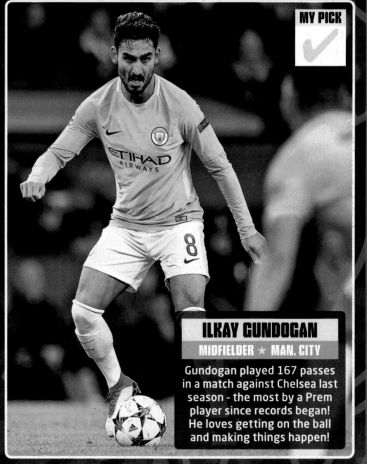

MY PICK ✔

ILKAY GUNDOGAN
MIDFIELDER ★ MAN. CITY

Gundogan played 167 passes in a match against Chelsea last season - the most by a Prem player since records began! He loves getting on the ball and making things happen!

HEADING

These heading heroes hardly ever get beaten in a one-on-one aerial battle!

MY PICK ✓

PETER CROUCH
STRIKER ★ STOKE

At 6ft 7ins tall, Crouchy has a big advantage in the air! Even though he only started half of Stoke's games last season, he still won more aerial battles than any other Prem player!

MY PICK ✓

CRISTIANO RONALDO
FORWARD ★ JUVENTUS

We can't think of a player with a better leap than Cristiano! He rockets himself into the air at a ridiculous speed, then uses his incredible thrust to bullet headers towards goal!

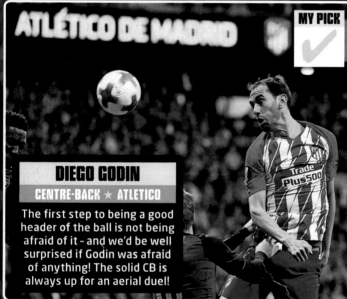

MY PICK ✓

DIEGO GODIN
CENTRE-BACK ★ ATLETICO

The first step to being a good header of the ball is not being afraid of it - and we'd be well surprised if Godin was afraid of anything! The solid CB is always up for an aerial duel!

MY PICK ✓

OLIVIER GIROUD
STRIKER ★ CHELSEA

Since joining the Prem in 2012, the France ace has scored tons of headed goals! His accuracy means he can steer the ball into the net from anywhere in the penalty box with his head!

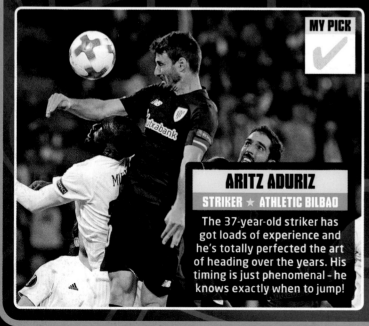

MY PICK ✓

ARITZ ADURIZ
STRIKER ★ ATHLETIC BILBAO

The 37-year-old striker has got loads of experience and he's totally perfected the art of heading over the years. His timing is just phenomenal - he knows exactly when to jump!

VISION

MY PICK ✓

ISCO
MIDFIELDER ★ REAL MADRID

Isco plays football like he's got eyes attached to a flying drone! His eagle-eyed vision means he knows exactly when to switch play or keep the ball where it is. He's unplayable!

MY PICK ✓

JAMES RODRIGUEZ
MIDFIELDER ★ B. MUNICH

James is one of the world's top dribblers - and that's down to the fact he's always looking up. He knows where the space is and can run into it himself or slip a pass to a team-mate!

MY PICK ✓

MESUT OZIL
MIDFIELDER ★ ARSENAL

Ozil switches assist mode to 'ON' when he scans the final third of the pitch for his next key pass! The fact he can then execute a perfect through ball takes him to the next level!

MY PICK ✓

LUKA MODRIC
MIDFIELDER ★ REAL MADRID

It's so important to have sick vision as a CM - you need to know what's around you at all times. That's why the classy Croatian is one of the best there is - his vision is epic!

MY PICK ✓

KEVIN DE BRUYNE
MIDFIELDER ★ MAN. CITY

We're convinced De Bruyne must have some sort of time machine, because the Prem's top assister in 2016-17 and 2017-18 always knows where his team-mates are gonna run!

POWER

When the footy skills wear off, these guys could have a change of career and join WWE!

MY PICK ✔

PAUL POGBA
MIDFIELDER ★ MAN. UNITED

Central midfielders use their upper body a lot to protect possession - and you'll see that watching Pogba. He's always using his strength to shield the ball from opponents!

MY PICK ✔

MOUSA DEMBELE
MIDFIELDER ★ TOTTENHAM

Whenever Spurs players get asked who's the strongest player in their squad, they always say the Belgium star! Opponents just bounce off him when they try to nick the ball!

MY PICK ✔

ADEBAYO AKINFENWA
STRIKER ★ WYCOMBE

Ade can lift around 200kg - double his own weight - which makes it impossible to get the ball off him on a footy pitch! He has his own cool clothing range too - 'Beast Mode On'!

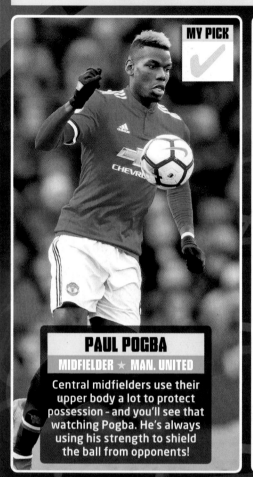

MY PICK ✔

SEAD KOLASINAC
LEFT-BACK ★ ARSENAL

Ex-Gunner Theo Walcott said Kolasinac was an 'absolute tank' - and that nickname has stuck among Arsenal fans! The tough Bosnian doesn't shy away from any tackle!

MY PICK ✔

ROMELU LUKAKU
STRIKER ★ MAN. UNITED

The Belgium beast must be a nightmare to play against! He uses his body to dominate defenders, push away and get a shot off at goal - that's why he busts so many nets!

TRICKS

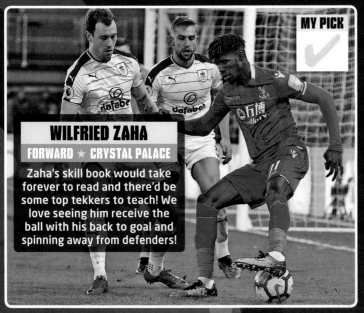

MY PICK ✔

WILFRIED ZAHA
FORWARD ★ CRYSTAL PALACE

Zaha's skill book would take forever to read and there'd be some top tekkers to teach! We love seeing him receive the ball with his back to goal and spinning away from defenders!

MY PICK ✔

MY PICK ✔

RICARDO QUARESMA
WINGER ★ BESIKTAS

Any match with Quaresma is worth watching just to see what tekkers he pulls off! His Rabona assist last season was sick and his Trivela goal at the World Cup was even better!

DOUGLAS COSTA
WINGER ★ JUVENTUS

As well as being the most successful dribbler in Serie A last season, Costa was also the most exciting to watch! Some of the skills he performs are just out of this world!

MY PICK ✔

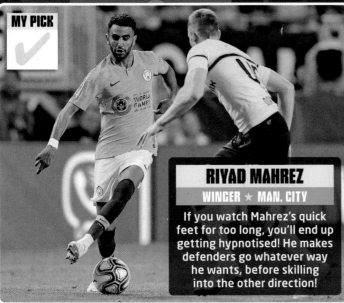

MY PICK ✔

RIYAD MAHREZ
WINGER ★ MAN. CITY

If you watch Mahrez's quick feet for too long, you'll end up getting hypnotised! He makes defenders go whatever way he wants, before skilling into the other direction!

NEYMAR
FORWARD ★ PSG

If you can name a trick, then Neymar can pull it off - he's got them all in his locker! But what we love most about the Samba star is how happy he is to try them out - he's so confident!

FREE-KICKS

These dead-ball demons absolutely love ripping the net from distance!

MY PICK ✓

MARCOS ALONSO
LEFT-BACK ★ CHELSEA

Alonso loves a bit of left-foot whip! The best example was his incredible effort against Bournemouth back in April 2017 – goalkeeper Artur Boruc stood absolutely no chance!

MY PICK ✓

PAULO DYBALA
FORWARD ★ JUVENTUS

The well classy Juventus and Argentina forward is all about technique over power. He once scored past a 20-man wall during a charity match in his hometown. Totally bonkers!

MY PICK ✓

KIERAN TRIPPIER
RIGHT-BACK ★ TOTTENHAM

Spurs supporters already knew exactly how good Trippier was from set-pieces, but after the World Cup the whole planet found out! His FK in the semis against Croatia totally rocked!

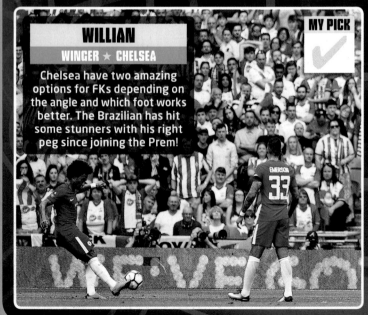

MY PICK ✓

WILLIAN
WINGER ★ CHELSEA

Chelsea have two amazing options for FKs depending on the angle and which foot works better. The Brazilian has hit some stunners with his right peg since joining the Prem!

MY PICK ✓

MARVIN PLATTENHARDT
LEFT-BACK ★ HERTHA BERLIN

The Germany full-back's first seven league goals were all free-kicks! He can knuckleball them into the net with such power that keepers shouldn't even bother trying to stop it!

HANDS

These goalkeepers are total legends when it comes to keeping the ball out of the net!

MY PICK ✓

MANUEL NEUER
GOALKEEPER ★ B. MUNICH

The Bayern Munich legend is known for being awesome with the ball at his feet, but he's also one of the best shot-stoppers on the planet - and has been for ages now!

MY PICK ✓

JAN OBLAK
GOALKEEPER ★ ATLETICO

Oblak's been Atletico Madrid's No.1 for the last three seasons and he's won La Liga's Zamora Trophy every time - the sick award for the lowest goals-to-game ratio. What a legend!

MY PICK ✓

HUGO LLORIS
GOALKEEPER ★ TOTTENHAM

The France and Spurs captain is a proper leader from the back and it helps that his team can totally rely on him! Lloris has got lightning-quick reflexes and super agility!

MY PICK ✓

DAVID DE GEA
GOALKEEPER ★ MAN. UNITED

The super Spain shot-stopper kept 18 clean sheets for The Red Devils last season, winning the Prem Golden Glove! No keeper had kept that many since Joe Hart in 2012-13!

MY PICK ✓

THIBAUT COURTOIS
GOALKEEPER ★ REAL MADRID

If you want your GK to boss the box with his height - Courtois is your man! The 6ft 6in Real keeper is the tallest option on this shortlist and can stretch to reach just about any shot!

FINISHING

Keepers don't stand a chance when one of these deadly hitmen go through on goal!

MY PICK ✓

CRISTIANO RONALDO
FORWARD ★ JUVENTUS

CR7 has evolved so much over the years! He started out as one of the most skilful, pacy dribblers on the planet and has now turned into the most prolific goal machine around!

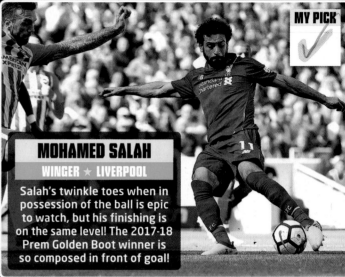

MY PICK ✓

MOHAMED SALAH
WINGER ★ LIVERPOOL

Salah's twinkle toes when in possession of the ball is epic to watch, but his finishing is on the same level! The 2017-18 Prem Golden Boot winner is so composed in front of goal!

MY PICK ✓

LUIS SUAREZ
STRIKER ★ BARCELONA

Uruguay have two epic goal grabbers in Suarez and Edinson Cavani, but it's the ex-Liverpool star that's won two European Golden Shoes - once for The Reds and once for Barça!

MY PICK ✓

ROBERT LEWANDOWSKI
STRIKER ★ B. MUNICH

Lewa's been absolutely lethal throughout his career, but his record for Bayern is just crazy! The Poland hero's netted over 40 goals in all competitions in the last three seasons!

HARRY KANE
STRIKER ★ TOTTENHAM

Kane established himself as one of the best strikers around in 2017, ending the calendar year with 56 goals for club and country - more than anybody in Europe's top five leagues!

MY PICK ✓

WORK-RATE

These lung-busters' batteries are always fully charged as they bomb around the pitch!

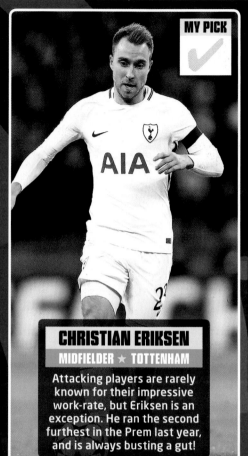

MY PICK ✓

CHRISTIAN ERIKSEN
MIDFIELDER ★ TOTTENHAM

Attacking players are rarely known for their impressive work-rate, but Eriksen is an exception. He ran the second furthest in the Prem last year, and is always busting a gut!

MY PICK ✓

N'GOLO KANTE
MIDFIELDER ★ CHELSEA

Kante's job in the Chelsea side is basically to cover as much ground as humanly possible – and he's no ordinary human! He runs all day, chasing down opponents and making tackles!

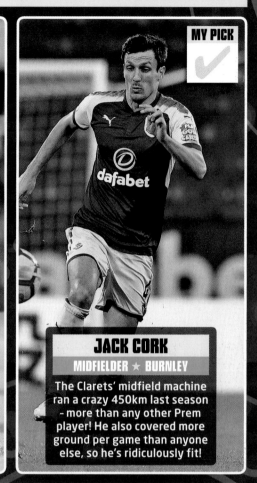

MY PICK ✓

JACK CORK
MIDFIELDER ★ BURNLEY

The Clarets' midfield machine ran a crazy 450km last season – more than any other Prem player! He also covered more ground per game than anyone else, so he's ridiculously fit!

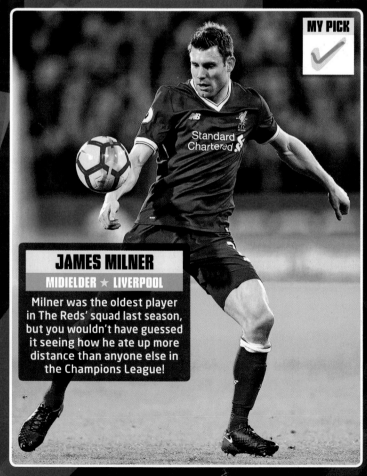

MY PICK ✓

JAMES MILNER
MIDIELDER ★ LIVERPOOL

Milner was the oldest player in The Reds' squad last season, but you wouldn't have guessed it seeing how he ate up more distance than anyone else in the Champions League!

MY PICK ✓

JORDI ALBA
LEFT-BACK ★ BARCELONA

Being a full-back is a tough job – you're expected to help out as much in attack as you are in defence! Not many do it better than Alba, who bombs up and down the left all game!

TACKLING

These stars make a living out of crunching into tackles and stopping attackers dead!

MATS HUMMELS
CENTRE-BACK ★ B. MUNICH

Bayern's boss at the back is a really composed defender – he never rushes into a challenge! Hummels patiently waits for the perfect moment, then strikes to nick the ball away!

MY PICK ✓

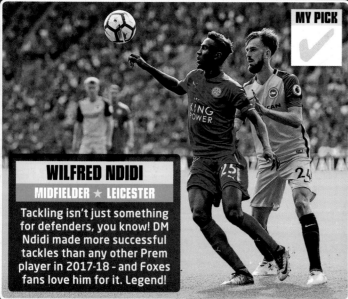

WILFRED NDIDI
MIDFIELDER ★ LEICESTER

Tackling isn't just something for defenders, you know! DM Ndidi made more successful tackles than any other Prem player in 2017-18 – and Foxes fans love him for it. Legend!

MY PICK ✓

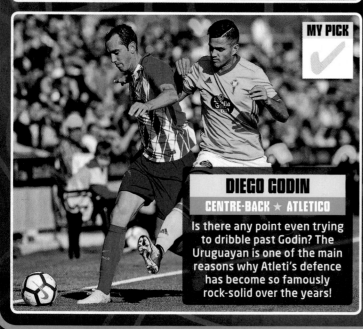

DIEGO GODIN
CENTRE-BACK ★ ATLETICO

Is there any point even trying to dribble past Godin? The Uruguayan is one of the main reasons why Atleti's defence has become so famously rock-solid over the years!

MY PICK ✓

SERGIO RAMOS
CENTRE-BACK ★ REAL MADRID

If there's one player strikers hate coming up against, it's Ramos! The Spain hero loves getting into a scrap and making monster challenges – and his timing is normally spot on!

MY PICK ✓

GIORGIO CHIELLINI
CENTRE-BACK ★ JUVENTUS

The best way to get past Chiellini is to knock the ball past him and beat him with pace. The CB has a top footy brain though, so he'll sit off you and still win the ball!

MY PICK ✓

BRAIN

These heroes are total footy geniuses when they step out onto the pitch!

MY PICK ✓

DAVID SILVA
MIDFIELDER ★ MAN. CITY

Next time you watch Silva, pay attention to how good his movement is! He always knows where he needs to be on the pitch to make sure he has the most impact!

MY PICK ✓

CHRISTIAN ERIKSEN
MIDFIELDER ★ TOTTENHAM

Some of the best playmakers are the cleverest footballers around – and Eriksen is defo one of them! He understands the game so well that he can dominate from anywhere!

MY PICK ✓

LIONEL MESSI
FORWARD ★ BARCELONA

On top of his incredible footy tekkers, Messi has a magical footy brain! His epic decision making means he always knows when to skin a man and when it's best to pass!

MY PICK ✓

JOSHUA KIMMICH
RIGHT-BACK ★ B. MUNICH

Being able to play right-back and in central midfield shows what an intelligent footballer Kimmich is. But the fact he can perform so well in both positions makes him a genius!

MY PICK ✓

JAN VERTONGHEN
CENTRE-BACK ★ TOTTENHAM

The 2017-18 PFA Team Of The Year CB reads the game so well. He always knows when a forward pass is coming, so he can step out first and nick it from the striker. Ledge!

DRIBBLING

Defenders totally dread one-on-one situations with these dribble kings!

MY PICK ✓

MOHAMED SALAH
WINGER ★ LIVERPOOL

Salah's dribbling style is similar to Lionel Messi's - the way he moves the ball forward mainly with his left foot, and then uses cuts to go inside or outside the defender!

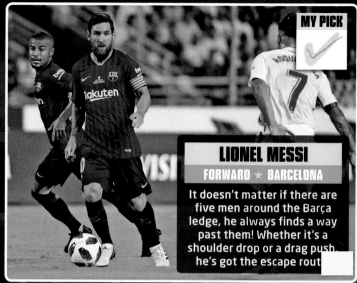

MY PICK ✓

LIONEL MESSI
FORWARD ★ BARCELONA

It doesn't matter if there are five men around the Barça ledge, he always finds a way past them! Whether it's a shoulder drop or a drag push, he's got the escape rout...

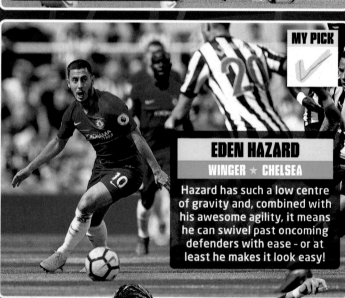

MY PICK ✓

EDEN HAZARD
WINGER ★ CHELSEA

Hazard has such a low centre of gravity and, combined with his awesome agility, it means he can swivel past oncoming defenders with ease - or at least he makes it look easy!

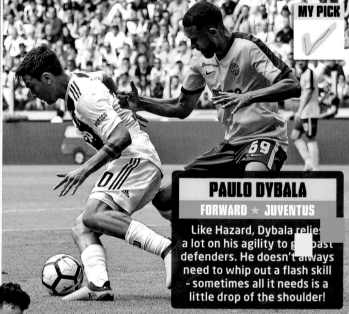

MY PICK ✓

PAULO DYBALA
FORWARD ★ JUVENTUS

Like Hazard, Dybala relies a lot on his agility to g... past defenders. He doesn't always need to whip out a flash skill - sometimes all it needs is a little drop of the shoulder!

MY PICK ✓

NEYMAR
FORWARD ★ PSG

If Neymar hasn't alread... ...ed the defender in knot... ...th his showboating, then he... finish them off with his dribbling! No Ligue 1 star completed more successful runs in 2017-18!

SPEED

These speedsters are like football's version of Formula 1 – they're absolutely lightning!

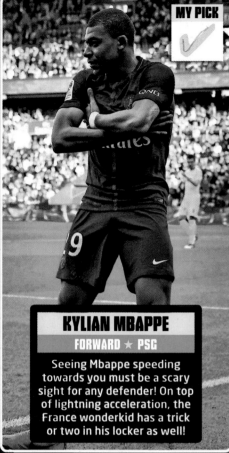

MY PICK ✓

KYLIAN MBAPPE
FORWARD ★ PSG

Seeing Mbappe speeding towards you must be a scary sight for any defender! On top of lightning acceleration, the France wonderkid has a trick or two in his locker as well!

MY PICK ✓

HECTOR BELLERIN
RIGHT-BACK ★ ARSENAL

We'd love to see a 100m race between Bellerin and Gunners team-mate Pierre-Emerick Aubameyang, because we're not sure who'd win! The full-back is absolutely electric!

MY PICK ✓

SADIO MANE
WINGER ★ LIVERPOOL

If Salah's got the skills and Roberto Firmino's got the link-up play, then Mane defo brings the speed to Liverpool's attack! The way he burns so easily past opponents is just mad!

MY PICK ✓

PIERRE-EMERICK AUBAMEYANG
FORWARD ★ ARSENAL

Knocking through balls to Auba makes total sense. Even if it's over-hit, the speedy forward will almost definitely latch onto it before anyone else - and then bust the net too!

MY PICK ✓

LEROY SANE
WINGER ★ MAN. CITY

Speedster Sane is definitely the Prem's version of Usain Bolt! The rapid winger clocked a top speed of 35.4km/h last season - quicker than any other player in the league!

BUILD YOUR ULTIMATE PLAYER

HEADING
MATCH PICKS:
OLIVIER GIROUD

YOU PICK:

VISION
MATCH PICKS:
KEVIN DE BRUYNE

YOU PICK:

POWER
MATCH PICKS:
ADEBAYO AKINFENWA

YOU PICK:

FREE-KICKS
MATCH PICKS:
KIERAN TRIPPIER

YOU PICK:

TRICKS
MATCH PICKS:
NEYMAR

YOU PICK:

FINISHING
MATCH PICKS:
CRISTIANO RONALDO

YOU PICK:

BRAIN
MATCH PICKS:
DAVID SILVA

YOU PICK:

WORK-RATE
MATCH PICKS:
JACK CORK

YOU PICK:

HANDS
MATCH PICKS:
DAVID DE GEA

YOU PICK:

SPEED
MATCH PICKS:
PIERRE-EMERICK AUBAMEYANG

YOU PICK:

TACKLING
MATCH PICKS:
SERGIO RAMOS

YOU PICK:

DRIBBLING
MATCH PICKS:
LIONEL MESSI

YOU PICK:

PASSING
MATCH PICKS:
TONI KROOS

YOU PICK:

WIN! EPIC PREDATORS

NAME:

DATE OF BIRTH:

ADDRESS:

MOBILE:

EMAIL:

BOOT SIZE:

Now build your Ultimate Player! Pick your stars, add your details, photocopy this page and send to MATCH. One reader will be picked at random to win a pair of adidas Predators, thanks to Sports Direct!

Post to: MATCH Annual 2019, Ultimate Player Competition, MATCH Magazine, Kelsey Media, Regent House, Welbeck Way, Peterborough, Cambs, PE2 7WH Closing date: January 31, 2019.

Fab Fact

Lingard has enjoyed loan spells at Leicester, Brighton, Derby and Birmingham!

Boots

adidas Nemeziz

Stat Attack

He's scored Wembley goals for Man. United in both the FA Cup and EFL Cup finals!

Transfer Value

£40 million

LINGARD

DRAW YOUR FAVE CARTOON!

If you love all the cool footy cartoons in MATCH, then you'll love this! Check out some of our faves, and draw a cartoon of your own footy hero for the chance to win an epic prize!

WIN!

Just photocopy this page,
draw your own footy cartoon
and post the drawing to:

MATCH Annual 2019,
Draw Your Fave Cartoon,
Kelsey Media, Regent House,
Welbeck Way, Peterborough,
Cambridgeshire, PE2 7WH

We'll then pick our favourite
picture and send the winner an
awesome Turtle Beach Recon
200 Gaming Headset. Get in!

Closing date: January 31, 2019.

Name:

Date of birth:

Address:

Mobile:

Email:

LIGUE 1 GOAL KING
CAVANI

Kylian Mbappe and Neymar grab a lot of the headlines in France, but when it comes to pure goalscoring, there's only one king of Ligue 1. Cavani has raced through the milestones to top PSG's all-time list of top scorers, and he doesn't look like slowing down any time soon!

GOALSCORING GAME

✓ Defenders hate playing against Cavani because he's got so much energy! He's always making clever runs to keep the centre-backs occupied!

✓ He doesn't just run away from his markers either. Cavani's got the height and strength to boss defenders and win tons of headers!

✓ Cavani's first touch rarely lets him down, so he only needs half a chance to control the ball before burying it past the keeper!

GOAL NO.1

PSG shattered their transfer record to sign Cavani for £55 million – and he didn't waste much time in showing his quality. In his first start v Ajaccio in August 2013, he collected the ball on the edge of the box, turned brilliantly away from his man and smashed an unstoppable strike into the top corner with his left foot. Worldy!

Club: *PSG*
Country: *Uruguay*
Age: *31*
Height: *6ft 2in*
Boots: *Nike Hypervenom*

FACTPACK!

BEST SEASON

PSG were sad when Zlatan Ibrahimovic left the club, but Cavani quickly made the fans forget about their former top scorer. After being given the chance to lead the line as the team's main striker in 2016-17, the Uruguay star had the best season of his career, slamming in 35 goals in just 36 games, and missed out on the European Golden Shoe by just two net-busters!

LAST SEASON

Cavani wasn't as prolific in 2017-18 as the season before, but it was still an ace campaign for him. He was Ligue 1's top scorer for the second year in a row with 28 goals, and helped bring the league title back to Paris. With Neymar and Mbappe joining PSG's attack, Edinson spearheaded one of the deadliest forward lines in European football!

RIVAL FOR THE THRONE
Radamel Falcao

Falcao would be much closer to Cavani's scoring record over the last few years if it wasn't for injury. He fired Monaco to the title in 2017, but he'll need to stay fit for a whole campaign to stand any chance of stealing the crown from the PSG star!

GREATEST GOAL

PSG	4	0	Bastia

October 19, 2013 This goal combined incredible footwork, brilliant finishing and tons of confidence! Cavani tied the defender and goalkeeper in knots before scoring from an impossible angle. Hero!

Stats correct up to start of the 2018-19 season.

BIG MATCH! QUIZ
EFL SPECIAL

YouTube STAR!

Name the lethal 2017-18 Championship top scorer who's taken the place of Chris MD!

MATCH MATHS!

Can you figure out the numbers then do the sums for full marks?

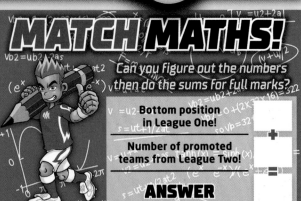

Bottom position in League One!	
Number of promoted teams from League Two!	**+**
ANSWER	**=**

THE NICKNAME GAME!

MATCH these wicked League Two teams with their class nicknames!

Crawley	Swindon	Crewe	Mansfield
1	2	3	4
A	B	C	D
The Robins	The Railway Men	The Red Devils	The Stags

FREAKY FACES!

Which on-loan Championship defender has been given a wacky makeover in this crazy pic?

GROUNDED!

Which League One club plays their home games at Bloomfield Road?

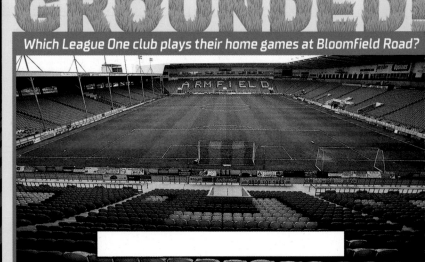

FOOTY MIS-MATCH

Spot the ten differences between these play-off pics!

1		6	
2		7	
3		8	
4		9	
5		10	

ANSWERS ON PAGE 94

EFL WORDFIT!

Fit these 30 EFL stars into this monster grid!

Akinfenwa	Hemmings	Morrison
Chambers	Henderson	Newton
Clarke	Hylton	Osborn
Dack	Jackson	Powell
Eaves	Kee	Prosser
Flint	Lansbury	Revell
Forestieri	Mannone	Rodriguez
Forshaw	Marquis	Waghorn
Grabban	Martin	Waterfall
Grigg	McNulty	Zoko

ANSWERS ON PAGE 94

MATCH!
THE BEST FOOTBALL MAGAZINE!

Fab Fact

Kun became Man. City's all-time top scorer in 2017 with his 178th goal for the club!

Boots

Puma ONE

Stat Attack

Amazingly, Sergio's wicked net-buster v Iceland at Russia 2018 was his first ever World Cup goal!

Transfer Value

£70 million

AGUERO

Legendary PREM No.10s!

ARSENAL

DENNIS BERGKAMP
10

The 'non-flying Dutchman' spent 11 glorious seasons as The Gunners' No.10! He scored 120 goals in 423 games in all comps, and some of his strikes were absolute worldies – including his mind-blowing finish against Newcastle in 2002, which was voted the Premier League's best goal in its first 25 years! His strike partnerships with Ian Wright and Thierry Henry were legendary, and he's one of the few players to have his own statue built outside Arsenal's Emirates Stadium!

CAREER PREM STATS

Games	315	Goals	87	Wins	186

BOLTON

JAY-JAY OKOCHA
10

Okocha was one of the most skilful playmakers of his generation, and is widely recognised as an all-time Nigeria legend! His tekkers were epic, which led to the saying, 'he's so good, they named him twice!' He joined Bolton back in 2002 and spent four seasons as their No.10, scoring a sick free-kick on the last day in 2003 to help The Trotters avoid relegation, guiding them to the League Cup final in 2004, and securing UEFA Cup footy for the first time in their history in 2005!

CAREER PREM STATS

Games	124	Goals	14	Wins	43

EVERTON

MIKEL ARTETA
10

Anyone who plays for Barça's youth team has top quality in their locker – and Arteta was no exception! After spells at PSG, Rangers and Sociedad, Arteta established himself as one of the best midfielders in the Prem! He was a top passer and a penalty expert, and after wearing No.6 for the first three and a half seasons at Goodison Park, he switched to No.10 for his final three seasons!

CAREER PREM STATS

Games	284	Goals	41	Wins	144

WAYNE ROONEY
10

United have had some legendary No.10s - Mark Hughes was one of their star attackers in the early '90s, Ruud van Nistelrooy broke tons of scoring records in the early noughties, and even David Beckham wore the No.10 for a season before making the No.7 jersey his own - but Wazza has to get the vote as United's most legendary No.10. He spent 13 seasons at Old Trafford, ten of which were in the No.10 top, and became the club's all-time leading scorer wearing it. Ledge!

CAREER PREM STATS

Games	491	Goals	208	Wins	284

WEST HAM

PAOLO DI CANIO
10

When it comes to pure football geniuses to have played in the Prem, Di Canio is right up there with the best! He was a controversial figure - he pushed over a referee while at Sheffield Wednesday and stopped play by catching a ball instead of scoring when a goalkeeper was injured in 2000 - but he was a real talismanic captain for West Ham. His passion was absolutely loved by the supporters, and no-one will ever forget his incredible scissor-kick volley v Wimbledon in 2000!

CAREER PREM STATS

Games	190	Goals	66	Wins	72

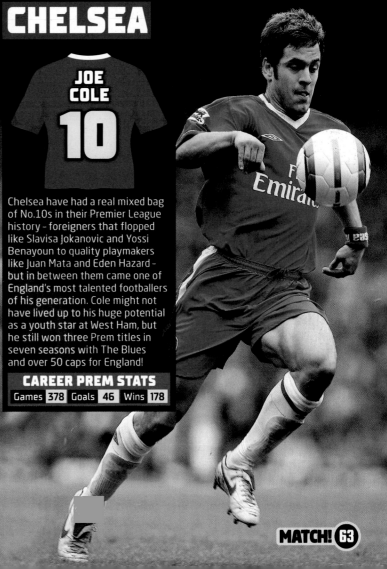

CHELSEA

JOE COLE
10

Chelsea have had a real mixed bag of No.10s in their Premier League history - foreigners that flopped like Slavisa Jokanovic and Yossi Benayoun to quality playmakers like Juan Mata and Eden Hazard - but in between them came one of England's most talented footballers of his generation. Cole might not have lived up to his huge potential as a youth star at West Ham, but he still won three Prem titles in seven seasons with The Blues and over 50 caps for England!

CAREER PREM STATS

Games	378	Goals	46	Wins	178

HARRY KEWELL
10

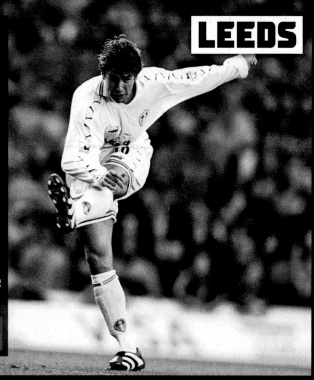

Kewell is probably the most gifted Aussie footballer ever, and before winning the Champo League with Liverpool, he was the star man of an electric Leeds team including Rio Ferdinand, Robbie Keane and Mark Viduka, which challenged the top four and reached the CL semis in 2001! He spent eight seasons at Elland Road, and in his first wearing the No.10 shirt, bagged 37 goals and assists combined in all comps!

CAREER PREM STATS

Games	274	Goals	57	Wins	131

SERGIO AGUERO
10

While most of the No.10s in this list are past Premier League legends, Aguero is a current legend still absolutely ripping it up! He's now in his fourth season wearing City's No.10 jersey - after enjoying four campaigns previously as their No.16 - and his City career is littered with record-breaking moments! Kun's goals-to-game ratio is better than any striker in the Prem's top 10 all-time top goalscorers list, and his title-winning strike against QPR in 2012 will forever be etched in the Premier League history books!

CAREER PREM STATS*

Games	206	Goals	143	Wins	133

*Stats correct up to the start of 2018-19.

ASTON VILLA

DWIGHT YORKE
10

A lot of fans will remember Yorke as a Man. United striker, but he played double the number of games for Villa between 1990 and 1998. He always had a big smile on his face, but when he got in front of goal he had a real killer instinct! He wore the No.18 shirt before being handed the No.10 at Villa Park, and had three prolific seasons - scoring 46 league goals - before being signed by United!

CAREER PREM STATS

Games	375	Goals	123	Wins	169

LIVERPOOL

GARY McALLISTER
10

McAllister was a classy CM who won the league with Leeds in 1991-92 and enjoyed an ace end to his Prem career at Liverpool, but at Coventry he was right at the top of his game. He was captain when they escaped relegation in 1996-97 by beating Chelsea, Spurs and Liverpool in the run-in - and he'll be remembered for his long shots and set-pieces!

CAREER PREM STATS

Games	325	Goals	49	Wins	124

COVENTRY

JUNINHO
10

MIDDLESBROUGH

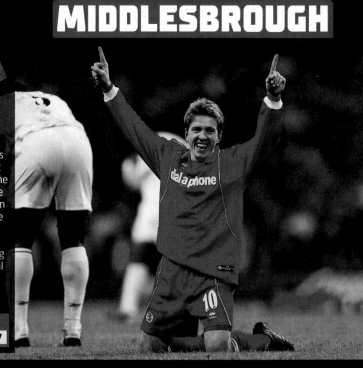

Juninho didn't play as many games as most stars on this list, but that didn't stop the baller becoming one of Boro fans' favourite players! He spent five seasons with the club, in three separate spells, and in three of those seasons wore the No.10. He was a typical Brazilian – flash tricks, top tekkers, demon dribbling and deadly free-kicks came natural to him - and he brought loads of flair and Samba style during his time at the Riverside Stadium!

CAREER PREM STATS
Games	Goals	Wins
125	29	37

MICHAEL OWEN
10

Owen is one of the quickest and most explosive strikers in England's history, and he burst onto the scene with Liverpool in 1997! He scored on his debut against Wimbledon, hit two epic hat-tricks for The Reds in his first full season and tore up the 1998 World Cup as a teenager for The Three Lions! Michael went on to play for Real Madrid, Newcastle, Man. United and Stoke, but it's his Liverpool and England career that cements his place as one of the best strikers of his generation!

CAREER PREM STATS
Games	Goals	Wins
326	150	142

TOTTENHAM

TEDDY SHERINGHAM
10

Teddy wore Spurs' No.10 from 1992 to 2003 - with four years squeezed in between at Man. United. He didn't have pace, but kept one step ahead of his man using his footy brain! He top scored in five of his seven Prem seasons at White Hart Lane, and formed lethal partnerships with Jurgen Klinsmann, Chris Armstrong, Les Ferdinand and Robbie Keane!

CAREER PREM STATS
Games	Goals	Wins
418	146	184

KEVIN PHILLIPS
10

SUNDERLAND

Phillips might have worn the No.10, but he played like a No.9! He spent six years with The Black Cats, four in the Prem, and formed a deadly 'little and large' strikeforce with Niall Quinn! He netted 113 league goals in 208 games, and also hit 30 goals in his debut Prem season to win the European Golden Shoe - the only Englishman ever to win it!

CAREER PREM STATS
Games	Goals	Wins
263	92	71

IF FOOTY STARS WERE...
EMOJIS!

We love footy heroes and can't get enough of Emojis, so we've combined both to see which stars best match the epic icons!

PUCKER UP

COME HERE, YOU!

SUAREZ SEES RED

NEVER A FOUL, REF!

LUIS SUAREZ
Barcelona

CALL A DOCTOR

MY HAIR STILL ROCKS!

OLIVIER GIROUD
Chelsea

MANUEL'S MOZZY MAYHEM

CHEEKY HAZARD

IT'S IN MY EYE!

MANUEL NEUER
Bayern Munich

TOILET TROUBLE

TAKE MY PIC!

EDEN HAZARD
Chelsea

CAN'T HOLD IT ANY LONGER!

JAVIER HERNANDEZ
West Ham

THUMBS UP

GONZALO HIGUAIN
AC Milan

YES, I'M IN MATCH!

KYLIAN MBAPPE
PSG

PUT YOUR HANDS UP!

SANE'S SHADES

LEROY SANE
Man. City

ROCKIN' RED DEVILS

LET'S DO THE DAB!

PAUL POGBA
Man. United

SAD ANDRES

I WANT MY MUMMY!

ANDRES INIESTA
Vissel Kobe

JESSE'S GEL GAFFE

MY HAND'S STUCK!

JESSE LINGARD
Man. United

SAMBA SMILES

WHO WANTS ANOTHER JOKE?

NEYMAR
PSG

BAD BREATH ALERT

DECISION TIME

MEAT FEAST OR VEGGIE HOT?

RAFA BENITEZ
Newcastle

CRANKY CRISTIANO

WHO SAYS LEO'S BETTER?

CRISTIANO RONALDO
Juventus

FORGOT TO BRUSH MY TEETH!

JORDAN HENDERSON
Liverpool

THE WORLD'S BIGGEST DERBIES

MATCH checks out the fiercest footy rivalries on the planet!

EL SUPER CLASICO
MEXICO

 CLUB AMERICA v **CHIVAS GUADALAJARA**

America and Chivas are Mexico's most successful teams ever and their rivalry is fierce! At the start of the 2018-19 season the two sides were tied on 12 league titles each, so the battle to be the outright kings of Mexican footy is on!

GRENAL DERBY
BRAZIL

 GREMIO v **INTERNACIONAL**

Brazil is a footy-mad country with loads of huge rivalries, but we had to pick this one as the biggest. While other cities like Sao Paulo and Rio de Janeiro are split between three or four teams, everyone in Porto Alegre supports either Gremio or Internacional, so when Gre-Nal clash the whole city's divided!

MEDELLIN DERBY
COLOMBIA

 ATLETICO NACIONAL v **INDEPENDIENTE MEDELLIN**

South America is the home of insane derbies and this is as crazy as any of them! When Nacional and Medellin play at their shared stadium Atanasio Girardot, the air is filled with the smoke from flares and 40,000 fans going bonkers!

SUPERCLASICO
ARGENTINA

 BOCA JUNIORS v **RIVER PLATE**

When Buenos Aires' biggest teams clash there are always fireworks! The whole city goes into meltdown ahead of a SuperClasico, and there aren't many games that can match its atmosphere. Most people reckon it's the biggest derby in the world!

URUGUAYAN CLASICO
URUGUAY

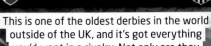 **NACIONAL** v **PENAROL**

This is one of the oldest derbies in the world outside of the UK, and it's got everything you'd want in a rivalry. Not only are they from the same city, Montevideo, they've also totally dominated the league title with almost 100 wins between them!

THE OLD FIRM
SCOTLAND

 RANGERS v **CELTIC**

The English Premier League might have more money, stars and quality, but Scotland still has the UK's biggest derby. Fuelled by passionate fans and total dominance over Scottish footy, the Old Firm is always totally explosive!

EL CLASICO
SPAIN

 BARCELONA v **REAL MADRID**

The most famous footy rivalry on the planet needs no introduction. It's not a local rivalry, but the battle between La Liga's biggest clubs usually features plenty of goals, drama and red cards - as well as the biggest and best players around! What more could you want?

DERBY DELLA CAPITALE
ITALY

 ROMA v **LAZIO**

There are more famous and more successful clubs in Italy, but no clash compares to the Capital City derby. The two sets of fans really don't like each other and it's often a bad-tempered derby - there's been 20 red cards in the last ten years!

INTERCONTINENTAL DERBY
TURKEY

 FENERBAHCE v **GALATASARAY**

Istanbul is divided in two, with Galatasaray on the European side and Fenerbahce in Asia. When they play each other, it's two continents clashing against each other, but there's footy on the line too. They've won 40 Turkish titles between them!

KOLKATA DERBY
INDIA

 EAST BENGAL v **MOHUN BAGAN**

India isn't known for its football, but this fixture is one of the biggest footy rivalries in Asia with tons of history. These two have been battling it out for almost 100 years and their fixtures regularly attract over 100,000 fans!

THE BIG BLUE DERBY
AUSTRALIA

 MELBOURNE VICTORY v **SYDNEY FC**

Until recently, the Australian league only allowed one team per city, so this rivalry became the country's biggest. It's known for bust-ups on the pitch and that's where it gets its name - in Australia 'a blue' is another word for a fight!

CAIRO DERBY
EGYPT

 AL AHLY v **ZAMALEK**

These two aren't just the most successful teams in Egypt, they're the most successful in Africa too with more African Champions League victories than any other team! That's taken their local city rivalry global!

SOWETO DERBY
SOUTH AFRICA

 ORLANDO PIRATES v **KAIZER CHIEFS**

These two teams are the most popular clubs in South Africa, so the country is well divided when the two local rivals take each other on. It always packs out the enormous 94,000-capacity Soccer City Stadium in Johannesburg!

BIG MATCH! QUIZ

EUROPEAN FOOTY SPECIAL

FOOTY AT THE FILMS!

Name the class La Liga full-back who's starring in the latest Jurassic Park film!

BACK TO THE FUTURE

Which Inter Milan ace has gone back in time to celebrate his side's 2010 Serie A success?

1.

2.

3.

🔍 SPOT THE SPONSOR!

Which European sides have these sponsors on their shirts?

4.

5.

6.

1.

2.

Beardy Weirdy!

Name the Ligue 1 megastars from their face fuzz!

3.

4.

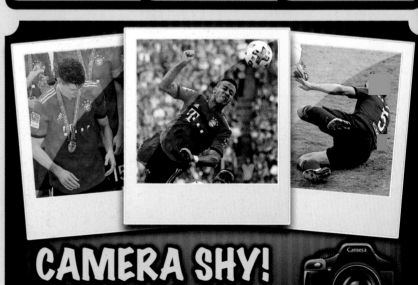

CAMERA SHY!

Spot the Bundesliga ballers hiding from the MATCH snapper in these pictures!

ACTION REPLAY

How much do you know about last season's Coupe de France final between PSG and Les Herbiers?

1 Which month was the epic season finale played – April, May or June?

2 What tier of French football were Les Herbiers in at the time – second, third or fourth?

3 True or False? This was the first time that these two sides had met in a cup final!

4 Did Giovani Lo Celso score PSG's opener in the first or second half?

5 How many yellow cards were there in total – under five or over five?

6 Which PSG ace sealed the win for the Ligue 1 champs late on from the penalty spot?

7 True or False? Both Les Herbiers' captain and PSG skipper Thiago Silva lifted the trophy together!

8 Which PSG superstar didn't play any part in the success – Kylian Mbappe, Julian Draxler or Neymar?

ANSWERS ON PAGE 94

CROSSWORD CRUNCH!

Use these clues to fill in MATCH's European footy crossword!

ACROSS

2. Number of Champions League titles Barcelona have won! (4)

3. Month that awesome PSG forward Neymar was born! (8)

6. Bundesliga top goalscorer in the 2017-18 season! (6, 11)

9. Main colour of Borussia Dortmund's home kit! (6)

10. Mega boot brand that Inter skipper Mauro Icardi wears! (4)

11. Brand that's designed Real Madrid's 2018-19 strips! (6)

13. Lethal Lazio striker that jointly won the 2017-18 Serie A Golden Boot! (4, 8)

14. Shirt number PSG hero Kylian Mbappe wore at the World Cup! (3)

16. Name of Inter and AC Milan's mind-blowing stadium! (3, 4)

19. Winners of the 2017-18 Dutch Eredivisie title! (3)

21. Boot brand that Lyon star Memphis Depay wears! (5, 6)

22. Number of league goals Timo Werner scored in 2017-18! (8)

24. Top goalscorer in Spain's La Liga in 2017-18! (6, 5)

25. Clubs relegated from La Liga in 2017-18 – Deportivo La Coruna, Las Palmas and _ _ _ _ _ _! (6)

DOWN

1. Premier League team Luis Suarez joined Barcelona from! (9)

4. La Liga side Spain midfield master Koke plays for! (8, 6)

5. Serie A club that went 18 league games without a win in the 2017-18 season! (9)

7. Prem side that Marseille's Florian Thauvin spent two years at! (9)

8. Country that Real Madrid ace Luka Modric plays for! (7)

12. Top assister in Germany's Bundesliga in 2017-18! (6, 6)

15. Sick Serie A team that lethal net-busters Dries Mertens and Lorenzo Insigne play for! (6)

17. Country that classy winger Iago Falque is from! (5)

18. Winners of the 2017-18 Portuguese league title! (5)

20. Name of Barcelona's massive stadium! (3, 4)

23. Italian club that signed Justin Kluivert from Ajax in 2018! (4)

ANSWERS ON PAGE 94

Fab Fact

In 2016, he finished third in the Ballon d'Or and won Euro 2016's Golden Boot and Best Player awards. Hero!

Boots

Puma Future

Stat Attack

Antoine's been Atletico Madrid's top goalscorer in each of his last four seasons. Goal machine!

Transfer Value

£90 million

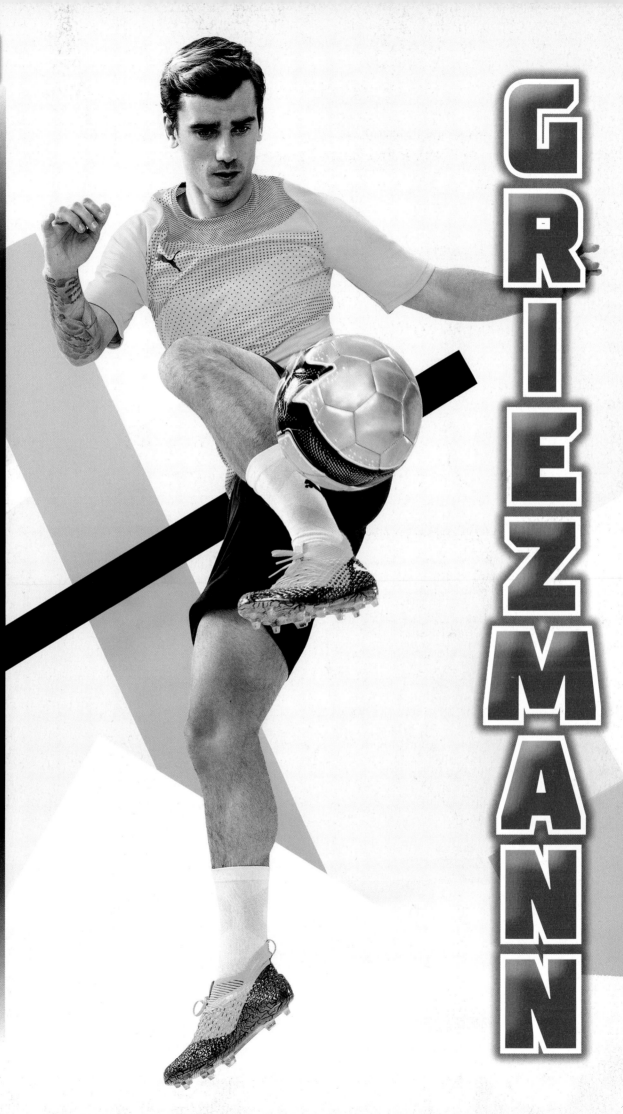

GRIEZMANN

SERIE A GOAL KING
ICARDI

Some players are just born to score goals and Argentina hot-shot Icardi definitely falls into that category. He's got the instincts of a true great and he keeps getting better and better every year. He topped the Serie A scoring charts in 2017-18 to become king of the league – and could reign for many more years to come!

GOALSCORING GAME

✓ Icardi is a penalty-box poacher! He's always in the right place at the right time to get on the end of chances and tuck them away!

✓ Almost all of the striker's goals come from one or two touches. He buries them in an instant, so defenders don't stand a chance!

✓ The Argentina superstar is ice-cool under pressure as well - that's why Mauro is so deadly from the penalty spot!

GOAL NO.1

Icardi bagged a classic poacher's goal in his first ever Serie A start in November 2012. With an ace run behind the Genoa defence, he raced onto a through ball and coolly slotted it past the keeper to seal the win. In their first season back in the top league, Sampdoria couldn't hold on to their star man for long and that summer Inter snapped him up for £6 million!

BEST SEASON

Nobody scored more Serie A goals than Icardi in 2017-18! After netting twice on the opening day, he never looked back and ended the season with 29 in total – every single one from inside the penalty box. Thanks to his goals, Inter returned to the Champions League for the first time since 2012, but the season ended in heartbreak when he was left out of Argentina's World Cup squad!

FACTPACK!

Club: *Inter*
Country: *Argentina*
Age: *25*
Height: *5ft 11in*
Boots: *Nike Hypervenom*

DID YOU KNOW?

Icardi started his career in Barcelona's academy, but left for Sampdoria to play first-team football!

THE 100 CLUB

In March 2018, Icardi became the sixth youngest player to score 100 goals in Serie A! He completed the century in style, bagging four times against his old club Sampdoria! Only two current players have hit more in the league, and don't be surprised to see Icardi overtake Gonzalo Higuain and Fabio Quagliarella very soon!

GREATEST GOAL

Inter	2	2	Bologna

April 5, 2014 Almost all of Icardi's goals are scored from inside the penalty box, so this was something really special! In one movement, the No.9 controlled the ball, spun and powered it into the top corner!

RIVAL FOR THE THRONE
Cristiano Ronaldo

When you hold the title of best scorer in your league, the last thing you need is CR7 joining it! The Juventus new boy wants to conquer Italy after bossing England and Spain, and there's a good chance he'll be the king of Serie A by the end of 2019!

Stats correct up to start of the 2018-19 season.

RUSSIA 2018
Scrapbook!

RUSSIAN STUNNERS!

The World Cup kicked off with a proper hammering! Sub Denis Cheryshev scored two screamers and Aleksandr Golovin added an epic free-kick late on as the hosts thrashed Saudi Arabia 5-0!

LIGHTNING LOZANO!

Mexico's pacy counter-attacking style stunned world champs Germany in their first game of the tournament, with Hirving Lozano's cool finish winning the game!

RONALDO TO THE RESCUE!

Portugal v Spain had absolutely everything - mistakes, drama, quality football and a stunning goal from Spain right-back Nacho! But Cristiano Ronaldo made the headlines by completing his hat-trick with a last-minute free-kick to seal a 3-3 draw. Wow!

COUTINHO CURLER!

This was meant to be Neymar's tournament, but Philippe Coutinho stole the show for Brazil! He scored an absolute worldy in their first game against Switzerland!

ENGLAND LEAVE IT LATE!

England's World Cup campaign began with a dramatic late win. Tunisia had drawn level with a penalty after Harry Kane's close-range finish, but the Tottenham man was on the spot to nod home again in the last minute!

KROOS CONTROL!

Germany looked set for another disappointing result in their second game, until CM Toni Kroos stepped up to a free-kick in the last minute. His curled shot gave the Sweden keeper no chance!

SHAQ & XHAK ATTACK!

Premier League heroes Granit Xhaka and Xherdan Shaqiri went nuts when their epic goals helped Switzerland come from 1-0 down to beat Serbia!

MAGIC MESSI!

When Argentina needed a goal against Nigeria to get them out of the group, Messi delivered! His first touch and finish were both absolutely world class!

SON STUNS GERMANS!

When Manuel Neuer went up the pitch to try to save Germany from losing to South Korea, everyone knew what would happen next. The keeper lost the ball and Heung-min Son sealed a 2-0 win to send the champions packing!

RUSSIA 2018
Scrapbook!

COUNTER-ATTACK KINGS!

Belgium sealed an incredible comeback in the last 16 with a devastating counter-attacking goal! Kevin De Bruyne, Thomas Meunier and Romelu Lukaku led the charge before Nacer Chadli finished it off to break Japan's hearts with a 3-2 win!

PAVARD PERFECTION!

France v Argentina was one of the games of the tournament! There were some unbelievable strikes in the seven-goal thriller, but Benjamin Pavard's swerving volley was the pick of them all!

HAPPY HOSTS!

Nobody expected Russia to even get out of their group, so when they knocked out one of the favourites Spain on penalties, the whole country went totally bonkers!

CAVANI SENDS C-RON HOME!

Uruguay strikers Edinson Cavani and Luis Suarez pulled off one of the best one-twos ever to open the scoring v Portugal, before the PSG striker added another to end Cristiano Ronaldo's World Cup dream!

ENGLAND END PENALTY HEARTACHE!

The Three Lions hadn't won a penalty shootout since 1996, and never in a World Cup, but an unreal save from Jordan Pickford helped them end that record against Colombia in the last 16!

BRAZIL BOSSED BY BELGIUM!

Kevin De Bruyne was the difference between these two quarter-finalists. His sick strike from the edge of the box was one of the Goals Of The Tournament – and left Neymar in tears!

CROATIA END RUSSIAN DREAM!

After a 2-2 draw, both Croatia and Russia went to a penalty shootout for the second time in a row to reach the semis, but the hosts' dreams were ended by Luka Modric and co!

GOAL

FRANCE REACH FINAL!

The first semi-final wasn't a classic, but Samuel Umtiti's dramatic header v Belgium took France to their second major tournament final in a row!

FOOTBALL'S NOT COMING HOME!

England fans had started to dream of the final when Kieran Trippier scored inside five minutes, but Ivan Perisic's equaliser and Mario Mandzukic's extra-time winner put Croatia there instead!

FRENCH GLORY!

The 2018 final was definitely one of the most dramatic and entertaining in years! Griezmann, Pogba and Mbappe added to Mandzukic's own goal to wrap up an awesome 4-2 win!

CRAZY WORLD CUP FANS!

What did this Peru supporter come as?

LIKE MY OUTFIT, MATCH?

OUCH, DUST IN MY EYE!

Japan's fans were praised for tidying up after themselves!

One South Korea fan got his flag stuck to his head!

SUPER GLUE PRANK!

When the footy ground in Russia served Balti pies!

YES... GET IN THERE!

We were wondering why Argentina legend Messi hadn't seemed himself!

SURPRISE, LEO!

WE LOVE HEADING BALLS!

Three Germany fans with three epic hat fails. Doh!

FUTBOL'S COMING HOME, OLE!

Mexico's fans did a good job of getting a tun out of their players!

THE THREE LIONS GOT 'ROBBED'!

Were these eye-catching WC fans auditioning for the new Power Rangers movie?

MATCH!
WEBSITE

Our awesome footy site features all this mind-blowing stuff...

WORLD STARS
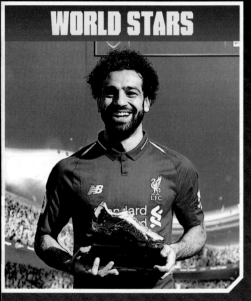

FIFA TIPS

EPIC VIDEOS
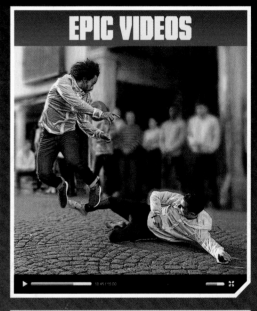

COOL QUIZZES

Who was the first keeper in the Premier League to make 100 saves in 2017-18?

Jack Butland

Hugo Lloris

David De Gea

Jordan Pickford

SKILLS ADVICE
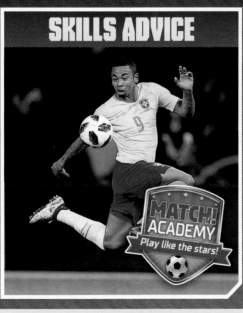

MATCH! ACADEMY
Play like the stars!

& LOADS MORE!
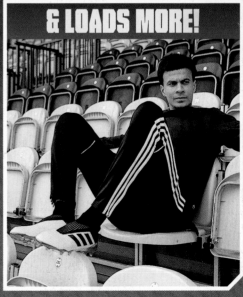

GO TO WWW.MATCHFOOTBALL.CO.UK

THE HIGHEST RATED FIFA TEAM EVER!

THIERRY HENRY
FIFA 2005
97

Striker

The Arsenal legend won the Premier League Golden Boot three years in a row between 2004 and 2006, and fired The Gunners to a Champions League final!

CRISTIANO RONALDO
FIFA 17
94

Left Winger

Ron and Lionel Messi have both had 94 ratings, but CR7 gets the nod in this team because Luis Figo plays in Leo's position. He actually overtook Messi as FIFA's best player in 2017!

MATTEO BRIGHI
FIFA 2003
97

Midfielder

Brighi was the best player on the game in 2003 and it's one of the great FIFA mysteries! He won Serie A Young Player Of The Year in 2002, but never fulfilled his potential!

ROBERTO CARLOS
FIFA 2002
92

Left-Back

Back in the early 2000s Real Madrid had the best players in the world in pretty much every position – and there weren't any better left-backs than Carlos!

FERNANDO HIERRO
FIFA 2002
94

Centre-Back

In 2002, Hierro won the Champo League for the third time in five years at Real Madrid – and that's why he bagged the joint-highest OVR ever for a centre-back. Total legend!

RONALDO

FIFA 2004

98

Striker

The lethal Brazil striker is back in FIFA 19 as an Ultimate Team Icon, but he's still not rated as highly as he was back in 2004. He was an unstoppable goalscorer!

The release of FIFA 19 means that EA SPORTS' epic footy game has been going strong for years. We've dug out our old copies of FIFA to reveal the best players to have ever appeared on the game, putting together this legendary line-up!

ZINEDINE ZIDANE

FIFA 06

96

Midfielder

Zizou's final year on FIFA was also his best! The Real Madrid and France playmaker was the best player on the game in 2006, but retired after that year's World Cup!

LUIS FIGO

FIFA 2002

97

Right Winger

The Real Madrid ace's dribbling and crossing ability made him one of the most dangerous wingers in the world in 2002. He was almost impossible to defend against on FIFA 2002!

GIANLUIGI BUFFON

FIFA 2005

97

Goalkeeper

The legendary Italian keeper is still going strong in FIFA 19 with PSG, but no GK has ever had a higher rating than his 2005 version when he was at Juventus!

ALESSANDRO NESTA

FIFA 2005

94

Centre-Back

AC Milan's Nesta was the best defender in the world in 2005 and he had the FIFA stats to prove it! His defensive and physical numbers were all in the high 90s!

LILIAN THURAM

FIFA 2005

92

Right-Back

With rapid pace, monster strength and rock-solid defensive ability, it's no surprise that Juventus' Thuram was rated so highly on FIFA 2005. He was a beast!

BUNDESLIGA GOAL KING
LEWANDOWSKI

With three Golden Boots in the last five seasons, Lewandowski has dominated the Bundesliga scoring charts for years – and the undisputed king of goal-grabbing in Germany has every skill required to carry on ruling over the league for a few more seasons yet!

GOALSCORING GAME

✓ Lewandowski is absolutely brilliant with his back to goal. Not only can he hold the ball up well, he's capable of spinning and shooting in an instant!

✓ When it comes to finishing, few players can match Lewa. He's got a rocket of a right foot and really smashes his shots when he gets a sight of goal!

✓ One of the Poland legend's trademark moves is volleyed goals. His technique is almost perfect when the ball is coming towards him in the air!

GOAL NO.1

Lewa became an instant Dortmund hero by scoring his first goal against massive rivals Schalke in September 2010. They were already 2-0 up when he powered a header past Manuel Neuer, and it was the first of many. He went on to hit over 100 goals for Jurgen Klopp's team, firing them to two league titles and a Champo League final, before joining Bayern in 2014.

FACTPACK!

Club: *Bayern Munich*
Country: *Poland*
Age: *30*
Height: *6ft 1in*
Boots: *Nike Hypervenom*

BEST SEASON

In Pep Guardiola's final season in charge in 2015-16, Lewa produced his best form. For the first time in his career he hit 30 goals, including five in one match against Wolfsburg. That proved key in clinching the Golden Boot – Lewa ended the season exactly five goals ahead of ex-Dortmund team-mate Pierre-Emerick Aubameyang and with another title in his cabinet!

DID YOU KNOW?

In September 2015, Lewa came on as a sub against Wolfsburg and hit five goals in nine minutes. Unreal!

LAST SEASON

He fell one short of the 30-goal mark, but Lewa was as clinical as ever in 2017-18, scoring every 75 minutes on average! In December he moved into the Bundesliga's all-time top ten goalscorers list and in March he became Bayern's top-scoring foreign player ever, too. Despite transfer rumours linking him with moves away, he's stayed sat on his throne in Munich!

RIVAL FOR THE THRONE
Timo Werner

After rival Aubameyang joined Arsenal in January 2018, Lewa's last challenger is speed demon Werner. He fired RB Leipzig to the Champions League in his first season in the Bundesliga and, at just 22, the Germany hitman has got big potential!

GREATEST GOAL

Bayern Munich	3	0	E. Frankfurt

April 11, 2015 This strike combined all of Lewa's best attributes – perfect positioning, fantastic first touch and a thumping volleyed finish. Top tekkers!

Stats correct up to start of the 2018-19 season.

#TRENDING

MATCH has picked out its favourite social media LOLs from 2018!

DISNEY WANNABE!

Marouane Fellaini had some bizarre hairstyles done for a photoshoot! Is that called, getting a Mickey Mouse?

CLAWSOME SNAPS!

Bayern posted some hilarious pics after their Champions League match with Besiktas got stopped because of a pitch-invading cat!

Dries Mertens ✓ @dries_mertens14 · 28 ene.
When someone farts in the stands 😂

Traducir Tweet

MEAN MERTENS!

Dries Mertens is a proper joker on social media, and MATCH loved this Tweet he sent after scoring!

💬 473   🔁 8,7K   ♥ 34K

MAN. CI-TEA!

Fabian Delph was well chuffed with his own brand of tea he received ahead of the World Cup in Russia! He said it was "better than winning the title!" Really?

Germany ✓
@DFB_Team_EN

Following ▾

Hey, @CardiffCityFC. Just letting you know, we have a really important tournament in the summer. Please don't hurt our players. Thanks, #DieMannschaft 🙏 #inSane

9:00 AM - 28 Jan 2018

SANE SHOCK!

Even the official Germany Twitter account must have been shocked Leroy Sane wasn't picked for the 2018 World Cup after they posted this back in January. Fail!

ULTIMATE PLAYER!

Why choose between footy megastars Cristiano Ronaldo and Lionel Messi when you can have them both on your back?

FUNNY TACTICS!

Who said Denmark relied on Christian Eriksen way too much at the World Cup? Well… this funny T-Shirt found in the country does!

WACKY RACES!

Is there a better way to prepare for matches than water unicorn races? The England boys don't think so!

Gladbach ✓ @borussia_en · 3 feb.
80 minutes gone, still goalless 😟

So @RBLeipzig_EN, tic tac toe?

🔄 Traducir Tweet

💬 144   🔁 4,7K   ♡ 7,6K

RB Leipzig English ✓
@RBLeipzig_EN

En respuesta a @borussia_en

Hmm, k.

10:11 - 3 feb. 2018

TIC-TAC-TOE!

RB Leipzig's match with Borussia Monchengladbach was so boring that their sides' official English Twitter accounts started a game of Tic-Tac-Toe. LOL!

CLASS KIT!

Hands down our favourite kit of 2018 was this Simpsons-inspired goalkeeper's jersey by Argentine side Ferro de General Pico. D'oh!

MATCH TACTICS (on t-shirt: Kick Off → Pass to Eriksen → Did he score? → YES / NO → DENMARK)

TOP 10 RECORD PREM SIGNINGS!

MATCH counts down the most expensive Premier League transfers of all time!

10 PIERRE-EMERICK AUBAMEYANG
£56 million ★ 2018
B. Dortmund to Arsenal

In 2013, Arsenal's transfer record was just £15m – miles behind the other big clubs – but then they finally shattered it! Mesut Ozil joined for £42.5m, then in 2017-18 they went totally berserk snapping up lethal strikers Alexandre Lacazette for £46.5m and Aubameyang for £56m!

9 AYMERIC LAPORTE
£57 million ★ 2018
Athletic Bilbao to Man. City

City spent nearly £100m combined on Kyle Walker and Benjamin Mendy in 2017, but that didn't stop them splashing big bucks on another defender just six months later! Laporte hadn't even won an international cap for France when he became their record signing!

8 ANGEL DI MARIA
£59.7 million ★ 2014
Real Madrid to Man. United

Chelsea's £50m signing of Fernando Torres stood as the British transfer record for ages before Argentina wing wizard Di Maria joined The Red Devils. His spell at Old Trafford was an epic fail, though – he left to join French giants PSG for £44m less than a year later!

7 ALVARO MORATA
£60 million ★ 2017
Real Madrid to Chelsea

Chelsea owner Roman Abramovich is famous for splashing the cash at Stamford Bridge, but it was taken to a new level when The Blues signed Morata in the summer of 2017! The jury's still out on whether the Spain star makes a success of his Prem career, though!

6 RIYAD MAHREZ
£60 million ★ 2018
Leicester to Man. City

Ever since Mahrez won the Prem title and PFA Player Of The Year award with Leicester back in 2015-16, there were rumous he'd be leaving the King Power Stadium. Arsenal, Real Madrid and Barça were all linked, before City swooped!

ALISSON

£66.8 million ★ 2018
Roma to Liverpool

Loris Karius' horror show in the 2018 Champions League Final made The Reds take drastic action! They nearly doubled the previous transfer record for a keeper – Ederson's £35m move to Man. City in 2017 – by paying Roma nearly £67m for Brazil No.1 Alisson. Wowzers!

5

KEPA ARRIZABALAGA

£71.6 million ★ 2018
Athletic Bilbao to Chelsea

4

Alisson's stint as the most expensive keeper ever lasted just 20 days, though! With Belgium's Thibaut Courtois on his way to Real Madrid, Chelsea activated Kepa's monster £71.6m release clause at Athletic to make him the new king of keepers!

VIRGIL VAN DIJK

£75 million ★ 2018
Southampton to Liverpool

3

Just six months before Liverpool broke the world transfer record for a keeper, they did exactly the same for a defender! Van Dijk had been linked with The Reds for ages before moving to Anfield for £23m more than previous record holder Benjamin Mendy. Crazy!

ROMELU LUKAKU

£75 million ★ 2017
Everton to Man. United

2

After busting 85 Prem nets for West Brom and Everton, Belgium beast Lukaku became the most expensive player ever to transfer between two British clubs when he joined United! Just a year later, he became only the 28th player to score 100 Prem goals too!

PAUL POGBA

£89 million ★ 2016
Juventus to Man. United

1

Pogba left Old Trafford in 2012 to join Juve on a free transfer, but after bossing Serie A for four seasons, United were determined to bring him back – even if it meant breaking the world transfer record to do so! #Pogback went viral on his Red Devils return and 'The Dab' was finally back at the Theatre Of Dreams!

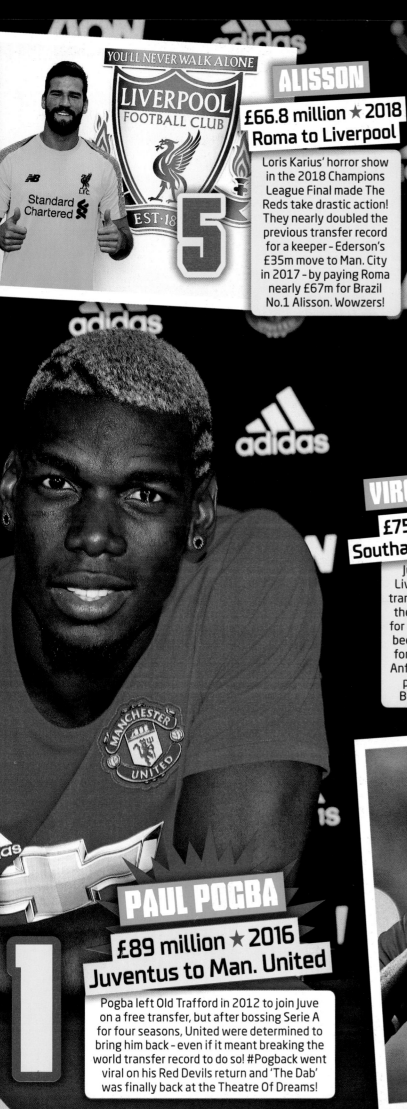

EXTRA-TIME

Reckon your footy knowledge is off the charts? Well, you can find out by tackling these mega tricky brain-teasers!

1 How many Premier League goals did Spurs star Harry Kane score in 2017-18?

2 Name the class midfielder that became the all-time leading Premier League appearance maker in 2017-18!

3 Which English club's awesome footy mascot is called Cherry Bear?

4 Which Spanish team used to play at the Vicente Calderon - Atletico Madrid, Athletic Bilbao, Valencia or Villarreal?

5 Which EFL side did Huddersfield sign tricky winger Alex Pritchard from in the 2018 January transfer window?

6 What is Championship club Millwall's awesome animal nickname - The Tigers, The Lions or The Leopards?

7 Which nation was the first to be knocked out of World Cup 2018 - Morocco, Saudi Arabia, Australia, Germany or Peru?

8 Which France superstar has got more followers on Instagram - Hugo Lloris, Benjamin Mendy or Antoine Griezmann?

9 Who has more all-time Premier League assists - James Milner or Wayne Rooney?

10 What country does Borussia Dortmund wing wizard Christian Pulisic play for?

11 Which English club did footy legend Michael Owen not star for - Liverpool, Man. United, Newcastle, Chelsea or Stoke?

12 Which of these mega stadiums has the biggest capacity - the Bernabeu, Old Trafford, London Stadium or San Siro?

13 Which of these isn't a recognised skill move in football - The Cruyff Turn, The Messi Twirl or The Bolasie Flick?

14 True or False? Burnley goalkeeper Joe Hart has his own waxwork at Blackpool's Madame Tussauds!

15 Which famous North London club does tennis legend Andy Murray support - Arsenal or Tottenham?

16 What is the Australian national team's wicked nickname - The Kangaroos, Footballroos, Socceroos or Strikeroos?

17 What position did legendary Germany international Oliver Kahn used to play?

18 How many teams compete in the German Bundesliga - 18, 20 or 24?

19 Which Milan rival finished higher in the 2017-18 Serie A table - AC or Inter?

20 True or False? The awesome Rabona skill was named after a famous Argentina striker called Angel Rabona!

21 In the 2017-18 Premier League season, were there more players wearing Nike or adidas boots?

22 Which classy playmaker completed more passes in La Liga in 2017-18 - Toni Kroos or Sergio Busquets?

23 Newell's Old Boys, Boca Juniors, River Plate, Independiente and Estudiantes all play in which South American country?

24 Which current League Two side hasn't played in the Premier League before - Swindon, Colchester or Oldham?

25 What year did legendary manager Sir Alex Ferguson retire from football - 2012, 2013 or 2014?

ANSWERS ON PAGE 94

LOVE MATCH?
GET IT DELIVERED EVERY WEEK!

15 FREE POSTERS

GOALS & STATS!

STAR MEN & MORE!

MATCH!

WORLD CUP POSTER PULLOUT

RUSSIA 2018 COOL POSTERS

★ 15 WORLD CUP STARS TO STICK ON YOUR WALL ★

COLLECT THEM EVERY WEEK!

POLAND

OWSKI

IT'S COMING HOME!

COOL

ENG

WE'RE SUPPORT

EYE-BUSTE

HUGE MATCH

COOL GIFTS

PANINI 2018 FIFA WORLD CUP RUSSIA™

RUSSIA 2018

EPIC PANINI STICKERS

5 STICKERS IN A PACK!

*Stickers may differ from those shown and will not be available overseas.

WORLD CUP 4 WEEKS TO GO!

MATCH!

MAY 15-21, 2018
ISSUE NO: 1974 ★ £2.59

9 770955 494988

FA CUP FINAL SPECIAL!

MAN UNITED

CHELSEA

PLUS 11 TEAM POSTERS

RE

WIGAN   MAN CITY

CHAMPS & PROMOTION!

101 TRANSFER RUMOURS!

ALL THE TOP GOSSIP REVEALED!

HOT GEAR

POGBA COLLECTION

NIKE WORLD CUP BOOTS

FIFA 18 WORLD CUP!

BIG NEWS INSIDE!

MORE! ★ UNITED v CHELSEA ★ NEW EVERTON KIT ★ INIESTA STATS ★ EUROPA LEAGUE FINAL ★ QUIZZES, FACTS & LOADS MORE!

Watford, Liverpool loads more new

PLUS

4 ISSUES FOR JUST £1!*

QUIZ ANSWERS!

Premier League Quiz   Pages 18-19

Odd One Out: Andreas Christensen.

Flipped: Marko Arnautovic.

Crazy Kit: Man. City.

Mega Mash-Up: Harry Maguire.

Stadium Game: 1D; 2A; 3B; 4C.

Spot The Ball: 13.

Guess The Winners:
2012-13 - Man. United;
2013-14 - Man. City; 2014-15
- Chelsea; 2015-16 - Leicester.

World-Class Keepers:
1. Burnley; 2. Everton;
3. Crystal Palace; 4. Bournemouth;
5. Man. United; 6. Tottenham.

MATCH Winner: Harry Kane.

Prem Wordsearch   Page 20

See below.

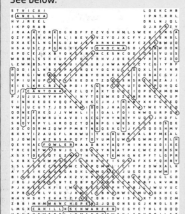

Champo League Quiz   Pages 32-33

Sport Switch: Neymar.

5 Questions On Bayern Munich:
1. Star Of The South; 2. Five times;
3. True; 4. Over 70,000; 5. No.5.

Close-Up:
1. Luis Suarez; 2. Joshua Kimmich;
3. Edinson Cavani; 4. Paulo Dybala.

Soccer Scrabble: Inter Milan.

Name The Team:
1. Sergio Ramos; 2. Toni Kroos;
3. Raphael Varane; 4. Karim Benzema;
5. Cristiano Ronaldo; 6. Casemiro;
7. Marcelo; 8. Dani Carvajal;
9. Isco; 10. Luka Modric.

Super Skippers:
Roma - Daniele De Rossi;
Atletico Madrid - Diego Godin;
Porto - Hector Herrera;
Monaco - Radamel Falcao.

Goal Machines:
1. PSG; 2. Schalke; 3. Napoli; 4. Roma;
5. Lyon; 6. Borussia Dortmund.

MATCH Winner: Roberto Firmino.

CL Spot The Stars   Page 34

See right.

EFL Quiz   Pages 58-59

YouTube Star: Matej Vydra.

MATCH Maths: 24 + 4 = 28.

Nickname Game: 1C; 2A; 3B; 4D.

Freaky Faces: Ashley Williams.

Grounded: Blackpool.

Footy Mis-Match: See above.

EFL Wordfit   Page 60

See below.

European Footy Quiz   Pages 70-71

Footy At The Films: Dani Carvajal.

Back To The Future: Ivan Perisic.

Spot The Sponsor:
1. Roma; 2. Inter Milan; 3. Juventus;
4. PSG; 5. Barcelona; 6. Bayern Munich.

Beardy Weirdy:
1. Dimitri Payet; 2. Danijel Subasic;
3. Adil Rami; 4. Dani Alves.

Camera Shy:
Robert Lewandowski, Thiago
Alcantara & Mats Hummels.

Action Replay:
1. May; 2. Third; 3. True; 4. First
half; 5. Under five; 6. Edinson
Cavani; 7. True; 8. Neymar.

European Crossword   Page 72

Across: 2. Five; 3. February; 6. Robert
Lewandowski; 9. Yellow; 10. Nike; 11.
Adidas; 13. Ciro Immobile; 14. Ten; 16.
San Siro; 19. PSV; 21. Under Armour; 22.
Thirteen; 24. Lionel Messi; 25. Malaga.

Down: 1. Liverpool; 4. Atletico Madrid;
5. Benevento; 7. Newcastle; 8. Croatia;
12. Thomas Muller; 15. Napoli; 17. Spain;
18. Porto; 20. Nou Camp; 23. Roma.

Extra-Time Quiz   Page 90

1. 30; 2. Gareth Barry; 3. Bournemouth;
4. Atletico Madrid; 5. Norwich; 6. The
Lions; 7. Morocco; 8. Antoine Griezmann;
9. Wayne Rooney; 10. USA; 11. Chelsea;
12. The Bernabeu; 13. The Messi Twirl;
14. True; 15. Arsenal; 16. Socceroos;
17. Goalkeeper; 18. 18; 19. Inter; 20.
False; 21. Nike; 22. Sergio Busquets;
23. Argentina; 24. Colchester; 25. 2013.

**Give yourself one point
for each correct answer!**

SCORE   /234